spiritual arts

spiritual arts

MASTERING THE DISCIPLINES
FOR A RICH SPIRITUAL LIFE

JILL BRISCOE

ZONDERVAN®

ZONDERVAN.com/
AUTHORTRACKER
follow your favorite authors

ZONDERVAN®

Spiritual Arts
Copyright © 2007 by Jill Briscoe

Requests for information should be addressed to:

Zondervan, *Grand Rapids, Michigan* 49530

Library of Congress Cataloging-in-Publication Data

Briscoe, Jill.
    Spiritual arts : mastering the disciplines for a rich spiritual life / Jill Briscoe.
       p. cm.
    Includes bibliographical references.
    ISBN-13: 978-0-310-27324-0
    ISBN-10: 0-310-27324-2
    1. Spiritual life—Christianity. I. Title.
    BV4501.3.B7545   2007
    248.4—dc22
                                                   2007000444

Published in association with the literary agency of Alive Communications, Inc., 7680 Goddard Street, Suite 200, Colorado Springs, CO 80920.

Interior design by Beth Shagene
Printed in the United States of America

---

07 08 09 10 11 12 13 • 22 21 20 19 18 17 16 15 14 13 12 11 10 9 8 7 6 5 4 3 2 1

I dedicate this book to all the people in prison
and in chains for Christ and his cause.
I pray that you will find the joy and exuberance
of the liberating power of the Holy Spirit,
so that your chains are no chains at all
but rather chains of blessing.
I salute you, marvel at you, and pray for you with Paul's words:

[I am] confident of this,
that he who began a good work in you
will carry it on to completion
until the day of Christ Jesus.

Philippians 1:6

contents

the art of spirituality

I like to think of the work of the Holy Spirit in the lives of men and women as art. Spiritual art. There are martial arts, culinary arts, dramatic arts, musical arts, fine arts—and spiritual arts. "Spiritual art" refers to the Holy Spirit's work in our lives—in character, gift, and blessing. There are the spiritual arts of intimacy, humility, serenity, harmony, and maturity. There is the art of spiritual tenacity too. There is God's part in this program, and there is our part. As the Holy Spirit does his transforming work within us, we must cooperate. We must give way to the Spirit's prompting, give in to his plans for our lives, and embrace the work he has for us to do. We need to *work out* what he is *working in*. There is just as much spiritual discipline needed on my part as the self-discipline needed for the rest of the arts. Just as I need to study the art of music and practice it, so I must study the art of humility and practice it.

I began to study and practice the spiritual arts at the age of eighteen, which is the age many of us are attending colleges or universities. Actually, I happened to be in both Cambridge University and the Holy Spirit's arts school at the same time. I soon discovered I would be in this spiritual schooling all my life, long after I had hung my Homerton College teacher's diploma on the wall in my office. This spirituality is a lifetime course, and you never graduate on this side of heaven itself.

When I was eighteen, I was into the dramatic arts, the entertainment arts, and the recreational arts. I wasn't much for the vocational arts—I was having too much fun. I was far too selfish to think about a career that helped anyone else, and I thought that the religious arts I'd heard about were weird and boring. I didn't know that religious arts aren't a bit the same as spiritual arts. That's because you need the Spirit to be spiritual, but you can be religious all on your own.

I was doing very well in all the arts I was taking, and above all the art of being totally selfish. But a totally self-centered life was not bringing me happiness. Fleeting pleasure, yes, but I couldn't master the art of being happy all the time, or even most of the time, no matter how hard I tried. I didn't know that contentment and joy are the Spirit's art, and are quite different from happiness, which usually depends on us getting our happenings happening the right way and stopping all trouble that troubles us. Seeing that we are not God, this is an exhausting and fruitless exercise. After all, it takes the Spirit of God to make it possible for us to be content and full of joy whether our happenings are behaving or not!

I had never heard of the spiritual arts, but then I had never heard of the Holy Spirit. I had, however, heard of the Holy Ghost. This was because we used to say the Apostles' Creed the old-fashioned way in school every morning. At the age of six, I had an experience in an air-raid shelter at the height of World War II that was the start of my journey home to God.

I didn't go to church, but I did know the creed from my school recitations. One night I prayed desperately to God the Father, God the Son, and God the Holy Ghost to stop the bombs. God didn't stop the bombs from falling. But as I prayed a six-year-old's desperate prayer in that dark underground hole, God answered in a different way altogether. He calmed the raging fear inside, wrapping my panicked heart in a peaceful blanket as surely as my mother wrapped me up in an earthly blanket as she cradled her frightened child in her arms.

It took twelve more years—until I arrived at Homerton College—to understand what happened in that air-raid shelter all those years ago. Twelve more years to hear about the university of faith and spiritual art and discipline, and about the Principal of that heavenly school, who was the Holy Spirit.

One incredible day, I got really sick, was rushed to the hospital, and lay frightened and alone in a large ward. Oh, there were other people there, about thirty or so, but you can be alone in a crowd, as I'm sure you know.

God came near in the person of a nurse, who was also sick and was a new believer. She was actually in the bed next to mine. She told me about Christ's work for me on the cross and how Jesus by his Spirit could invade my life, forgive my sin, and save my soul. I believed as soon as I heard the story of Jesus and his love, and I discovered that the Spirit had enrolled me in a lifetime course of his arts.

One of the Bible books that best summarizes these arts is Paul's letter to the Philippians. When Paul wrote to the Philippian believers, he instructed them in much of what they (and we) should know about living out the spiritual arts.

THE BIRTH OF THE PHILIPPIAN CHURCH

Paul wanted to go to Asia and preach the gospel. He had a team of missionaries with him—young Timothy, his "true son in the faith" (1 Timothy 1:2), and Dr. Luke, who became the journalist and historian in the group. Luke joined Paul's party and began to write in the personal tense ("we" did this or that), and this is how we know when he joined up with the party. You can read his account of what happened in Acts 16. He was with the group when they went to Philippi.

One night Paul had a vision. He saw a man of Macedonia begging, "Come over to Macedonia and help us." In the morning, Paul was so sure God had given him this vision that he shared it with the others, and they decided to change their plans immediately and head out to Europe. They believed that the Spirit of God was guiding them to the right place to go.

When they arrived in Philippi, they waited for a day or two, no doubt waiting for the man in Paul's vision to show up. Apparently he didn't appear, and so the men went to find a group of Jews who, they suspected, would be meeting by the river on the Sabbath. When they found the worshipers, there were no men, but they did find a woman named Lydia—a wealthy merchant woman, a seller of purple cloth—and God opened her heart to the gospel. Paul was only too eager to share. She insisted they come back to her house, and so the church in Philippi began.

A LETTER TO A STRUGGLING CHURCH

Years later, at the end of his life, Paul heard of struggles in the Philippian church. He loved the church dearly and would have visited it, except for one small problem—he was in prison, probably in Rome. So he wrote a letter instead.

Writing letters is an art—a dying one since the computer took over the world. Who keeps emails these days, tying them up in ribbons and leaving them behind for the children to sift through when we're gone? The other day as I was cleaning out a closet, I came across a bundle of letters my husband had sent me when we first fell in love. They were love letters—wonderful letters telling of the incredible discovery of each other in delight and excitement as God introduced us to each other and said, "Enjoy!" I cried my way through them. I decided to divide them up for my children so they can have part of their heritage. After all, if it were not for the love that these letters speak of, David, Judy, and Pete would not even exist.

But writing letters can be a spiritual art as well. If it were not for the wonderful letters of love from Paul's quill in the first century, I wonder how many of God's children would exist today? How wonderful that someone kept Paul's epistles for us as part of our inheritance!

A PERSONAL LETTER — AND SO MUCH MORE

What kind of letter is Philippians? First, the letter to the Philippians is a *preserved* letter—a letter inspired by the Holy Spirit and preserved by the Spirit for today's believers.

Philippians is also a *personal* letter. When the letter came to Philippi, it was read to the church, a group of people who lived in Philippi and who had originally become Christians through Paul's ministry. They probably met in a home, in this case, perhaps Lydia's.

The letter is a *practical* letter. Paul, dealing with the practical issues of faith, teaches the Philippians how they can apply spiritual principles to everyday living—for example, how to be happy when you're sad all the time (such as when you're in prison), how to use bad times to good ends (such as spreading the gospel to the guard who can't get away because he's chained to you), and how to get along with difficult people (such as fellow church members).

It's a *political* letter—political in the sense that it tells us a little of what was going on in the Roman Empire, such as the persecution of Christians. Paul is awaiting trial in jail, probably in Rome. He is in this predicament because of his faith—a regular happening for Paul.

It is a *prison* letter. Paul wrote a few letters from prison. I call them "jail mail." My husband jokes, "When Paul first went to a city, he liked to check out the jail, as he knew he would probably end up there sooner or later."

It is a *powerful* letter. It is pure spiritual art. It can change your life if you read it on your knees and allow your heart to be transformed by its truths. It can tell you how to "keep on keeping on" when you're just about done with the whole thing—discouraged, disappointed with people, and fed up with life.

It's a *prayerful* letter. It starts and ends with prayer. It provides us with great ideas for prayers that work, and all of us want that. Paul even wrote out a prayer in the letter, so we can now borrow his own words to get us started.

It's a *praiseful* letter, and that is the amazing thing about the Philippians letter: it is the epistle of joy! Joy laces the words together, tying it into the God of the universe, whose nature is unspoiled joy spilling over into our hearts, even when we are old and lonely, manacled in a filthy, dark cell awaiting possible execution. I want to know how a life like that is possible—don't you?

Paul may well have been incredulous that two thousand years after his death, his letter had found its way into the Bible, to be read in every nation where the gospel has been preached, translated into hundreds of languages, and used to make Jesus-lovers out of us all. So read Philippians, and open your heart and mind to the arts of the Spirit through Paul, a "servant of Christ Jesus" (Philippians 1:1).

CHAPTER 1

the spiritual art of
ministry

Whatever happens, conduct yourselves
in a manner worthy of the gospel of Christ.
Philippians 1:27

People often say to me, "I wish I knew what God wanted me to do with my life."

"That's easy," I reply. "Ministry."

Their eyes open wide. "You mean give up my job and go away to a nunnery or something?"

"No," I reply, "probably not. Just get going. Look around you. The mission field is between your own two feet at any one time."

Ministry is not something for the professional Christian only—someone who has been to seminary or Bible school or on the mission field. It is for all who have become new persons in Christ Jesus and have experienced "the old things passing away, and all things becoming new" (see 2 Corinthians 5:17 KJV). It is for those who have had a radical change in their lives because of their conversion and who want—more than that, *feel*—a responsibility to make sure everyone has the same opportunity.

Ministry is being a blessing. It's serving and giving and not counting the cost. It's what we who love Jesus are supposed to be doing all day, every day. Ministry is talking about Jesus, serving Jesus, being Jesus where people are in need of Jesus. Ministry is the most exciting, stretching thing in the world. It's an art — a spiritual art.

Ministry — helping people — happens all day every day and all night every night. Ministry goes on all over the world and on all seven continents. Old people and young people minister. Black people and white people. Wealthy people and poor people. Sick people and healthy people. Ministry is a full-time twenty-four-hour thing. An "I can't wait to get going in the morning" thing. An "I don't have time to sleep" thing. An "I can't believe I have the privilege of doing this" thing. It's a hard thing, a glorious thing, a stretch, a reach, a "pulling you in every direction" thing. It is exhausting and exhilarating, an emptying of yourself and a "filling up to overflowing" thing. Ministry is in the end an art of the Spirit — a spiritual art.

A CHAIN OF BLESSING

Christian ministry is a chain of blessing that begins with someone getting blessed — someone coming to faith in Jesus Christ and being converted, turned around, transformed from the inside out — and in turn being a blessing to everyone in their orbit. It's a chain. A chain of blessing.

When I was converted, the girl who led me to the Lord handed me a Bible and told me to start reading it and to share my discoveries with everyone in sight. Seeing that I was in the hospital at the time and she was sick in the bed next to me, I looked at her inquiringly, suspecting she actually meant for me to share with all the people in the ward and the nurses, doctors, friends, and family members who came to visit. She did.

"Look," she said, pointing to a starched and somewhat formidable woman, "the chief nurse is coming. Tell her what you've just told God when you prayed with me."

Before I could protest, the nurse was at my bedside, and conscious of the eagle eye of my spiritual mother on my every move, I prayed my second prayer (the first had been prayed a brief time before, when I had invited Christ into my life) and wondered what on earth I was going to say. I needn't have worried.

"What's this?" asked the nurse, picking up the Bible that had suddenly appeared on my bedside table.

"Uh, a Bible," I answered somewhat lamely. She shot me a look I couldn't read—or rather didn't want to interpret, because I knew she had heard my crude language and seen my wild friends visiting me and was obviously thinking, "Oh my, this is a change of personality; she needs the psychiatrist"—and she did actually send one to see me that afternoon!

Janet, my new friend, had told me about Jesus, and now I told the nurse about him as best I could. I did an awful job of it, of course. I was less than a few hours old—a baby Christian—but something happened to me as I confessed my very new faith to her. I didn't know then that the Bible said I was to believe in my heart and make confession with my lips about my salvation (Romans 10:10), but spurred on by Janet, I obeyed.

I remember looking at the startled nurse and seeing a rather hard woman who was worried about something, who didn't know she needed a God to lean on, a Christ to save her, and some peace of mind. In my tiny way I put a link on the chain. *And I got it.* This was it. I was to be part of chains of blessing for the rest of my life. I was to learn this spiritual ability, this spiritual art of ministry.

Of course, I realized at once that I had a lot to learn. It would take a lot of expertise to lead this woman to Jesus as Janet had led me, and for that I would need to go to some sort of school, I supposed. It was Janet who told me that I was enrolled already in the school of spiritual arts, and the Spirit himself would show me how to minister. It was also Janet who showed me that I would have opportunities every day to practice ministry. She opened my eyes to the opportunities 24–7, as they say.

"Wake up in the morning, Jill, determined to be a blessing," Janet had said. I should have this attitude, whether people wanted me to be a blessing or not. *This* was conversion. I who had woken up most mornings determined to be a bane was now to wake up determined to be a blessing? Well now, that would surely get my friends' attention. It did.

So ministry is for *all* of us — those of us who have grown up in the church and those of us who, like me, have come to Christ from the outside of "Christian everything." So don't say, "But I don't have any opportunity to minister. I have no training." Ask God to show you the hundreds of opportunities that are right under your nose every day.

MINISTRY IN DIFFICULTIES

Some people see a difficulty in every opportunity, while others see an opportunity in every difficulty. It's a question of the way you look at life. Something unfavorable happens to us that we are not expecting — how do we handle it? The book of Philippians is a marvelous book that gives us good examples of how to take advantage of trouble for God.

Sitting in a cold, dark jail cell, Paul wrote to his friends in Philippi: "What has happened to me has really served to advance the gospel" (1:12). He declares that *because* of his chains (1:14), he has this marvelous opportunity. He may as well have said "in spite of" my chains. Paul considered himself a prisoner not of Rome but of Jesus Christ. He was there as an ambassador to represent his Lord and Savior. Hadn't the Lord said, "I will show him [Paul] how much he must suffer for my name" (Acts 9:16)? God had also promised Paul that he would one day take the gospel to Rome, the heart of the empire (see Acts 23:11). When something hard happened to the apostle Paul, his instant reaction was, "How can I use this as a platform to explain the gospel?"

Paul had no idea how he was ever going to get to Rome. But he knew that one way or another, God would get him to the heart of the empire. And what would happen when he got there? Perhaps Paul envisaged a great crusade in the Coliseum. I doubt it though. He didn't know how this trip to Rome would actually happen and probably thought it could happen only if he were a free man. But Paul had a wonderful habit of seeing an opportunity to minister in every difficulty.

Paul, therefore, looked at his chains as a positive. "These are chains of blessing," he would have said to himself. In fact, he didn't just say it to himself; he said it to his friends: "These chains on my wrists have turned out to be chains of blessings for others." What an attitude! And Paul wants *them* to learn the lesson too. In another letter, Paul tells the Christians to make sure they learned to "make the most of every opportunity" (Ephesians 5:16). He wanted them to begin to practice the art of ministry.

Whether we find it easy or difficult to take the opportunity to make Christ known when we're in tough situations may have something to do with our personalities. It may be harder for some than others. I am a negative sort of person to begin with, while my husband Stuart is the positive part of the partnership. He would see the doughnut; I would see the hole. And if perchance Stuart would see the hole, he would spell it w-h-o-l-e. But faith can turn even a melancholy person into a positive one. To discover this was a huge encouragement that helped me see even confining situations as a chance to practice this spiritual art.

As we meet Paul in prison, most likely in Rome, there is little encouragement for him on the horizon. He is preparing to defend his life in a Roman court. He is to be put on trial for his faith, and he is not really expecting to win his case. However, he is quite at ease, as his faith tells him that if God wants him around a bit longer for the good of the young believers, he will be released. If not, he will walk through the front door of heaven and be with Jesus. He can't quite make up his mind which he prefers. He reckons he'd rather have heaven, but he's quite content to stay a while longer on earth for the sake of his beloved Philippians. "For to me, to live is Christ and to die is gain," he writes in his letter (1:21). You can't beat an attitude like that.

Shakespeare's Hamlet, prince of Denmark, would at a particularly dark time in his life walk around the ramparts of his castle with the same musings but draw quite a different conclusion. "If I live, it's awful; and if I die, it's worse!" he mused—or in other words, "To be or not to be: that is the question." Paul, on the other hand, was thinking about the same alternatives in front of him and saying to himself, "If I live, it's all about Christ; and if I die, I'll be with him forever. So keep me alive or kill me, no problem; take your pick."

A Christian has two great opportunities: to live and to die. Do you think of living and dying as two grand-slam opportunities? Well, it all depends on whether Christ is in your life. And if Christ is in your life, then death is your gain!

Back at the ranch, or rather at the jail, Paul was making the most of things. He was busy using his unusual opportunities and exercising the spiritual art of ministry.

THE MINISTRY OF PRAYER

Shortly after finishing school and beginning to teach in my hometown of Liverpool, I was rushed to the hospital by ambulance with suspected appendicitis. On the way, I thought to myself, "Well, I may be able to witness to some patients or nurses while I'm there." Then I thought, "But it's a good chance to catch up on my reading, or just relax as best I can and concentrate on getting well. Christians are allowed a little time off, aren't they?"

An idea intruded into my thinking at this point. What if Janet had spent her time in the hospital looking after only her own interests and had never had time for Jill Ryder? What if she had been solely absorbed with her considerable pain and not been amazingly able to reach out of it into mine? What if she hadn't prayed for me?

So I do remember realizing that I had an opportunity to exploit this difficulty for the Lord, just as Janet had used hers. But I don't remember thinking, "Yeah! This is a great chance to spend hours and hours in prayer for other people." But then I had not fully realized that taking every opportunity for Christ doesn't only mean talking to people but also involves praying for them. When trouble comes, we need to train our minds to go to God first and foremost in prayer, and then to keep on going.

A friend sent me a get-well card that said, "The world says, 'laid aside for illness.' Christ says, 'called aside for stillness.'"

"Bother," I remember saying out loud. I didn't want to hear that. I knew it was right, however, and so I told God I was sorry and began to use the hours I would have used talking to everyone and their wives who came on by or catching up on magazine gossip to learn the spiritual art of intercession. Chained to my hospital bed for a couple of weeks, my prayer life took a giant leap forward.

Now, we can pray anywhere, anytime, but sometimes we need a nudge to remember that. Circumstance can lend us a hand. After he gives his greeting, Paul is found in the opening lines of his letter praying for his friends, and he tells them so.

"I am praying for you," he says. He has had hours and hours of uninterrupted time in his cell to talk to his heavenly Father about his friends and their troubles. If he had been free, it wouldn't have been so easy to make the time. True, he is uncomfortable, and a guard is attached to him at all times of day or night—but no matter, it is downtime!

The prayer in Philippians 1:3–11 is fascinating. It tells us much about Paul. Paul's prayer isn't first filled with a list of prayer requests for his health or laments about the conditions "inside," though elsewhere in the letter he does ask people to pray specifically about his practical and personal needs, but Paul shows us here the heart of prayer by telling the Philippians that they are the focus of his thinking.

"I thank my God for you," he says. "I remember you—all of you—with joy all the time." He tells them what a sheer joy they are to him. So often we pray for people, and there's not too much joy in the doing of it. What a boost to our own faith when someone is bringing us joy, and how it encourages us to keep on praying for those who make our hearts smile.

Paul tells them that he believes in them and in the work of God within them that will continue in their hearts and lives to the end. He has confidence that they will stay the course. This isn't a reason to stop praying for them, he says, but a good reason to redouble his efforts. He is well aware that the Devil will not be idle when he sees people such as the Philippians finishing strong.

Someone once said to me, "You seem so strong that I don't feel the need to pray for you as much as for those who are weak." That didn't make me feel very safe! Paul knows that the Philippians are strong, but this is all the more reason to go on praying for them. He tells them that he loves them, misses them, and is homesick for them all (1:8).

Paul's intercession tells us about his relationship with the Gentile believers, and how deeply he loves the people he prays for. "I have you in my heart," he tells them (1:7). It always helps—loving the people you are praying for, having them in your heart.

Ask God to put the people you pray for in your heart. Ask the Spirit to transfer a piece of his heart for them to your heart. Loving someone will help you to keep your mind on others and off yourself and your own problems when you pray. And what does Paul pray for his friends?

First, he prays that their love for each other will grow and abound "more and more" (1:9). We all need more and more love for each other. Do you have anyone in your life that needs more and more love for others? I do. Pray "more and more love" prayers for them. Then Paul prays that they will know and discern what is best, and that they will live godly lives. He prays they may be people of integrity—Christlike—and that comes from the Spirit. Being like Christ is pure spiritual art. Lastly, Paul prays that God will get a lot of credit for the lives lived for him in Philippi. If you don't know what to pray for the people you love, borrow Paul's words or the pattern of his prayers.

Think about all the opportunities you've had this week to exercise the art of intercession for your friends. Unexpected times. Did you do it, or were you and the people in your heart poorer as a result of the lost opportunity?

THE MINISTRY OF EVANGELISM

Paul casually mentions that he is practicing the art of evangelism in jail. He writes, "What has happened to me has really served to advance the gospel. As a result, it has become clear throughout the whole palace guard and to everyone else that I am in chains for Christ" (1:12–13).

There are some situations we do not choose for ourselves where we find ourselves chained to a person, situation, or circumstance that is downright difficult or discouraging—or worse, dangerous. What will we do with them? Will we see the person or persons on the other end of the chain getting blessed? It's up to us. I ask myself, "In what way has what has happened to me advanced the gospel?" Or to put it another way, "What happened *through* me when something happened *to* me?" For example, did I miss the opportunity when I was in the hospital not only to pray for those in my heart but to evangelize as well? The hospital is a great place to talk about the Lord. People are a little scared, or at least apprehensive and certainly vulnerable, and we should take full advantage of it for the Lord.

In my case, I was in the hospital when I gave my life to Christ. I had never been in the hospital before and was scared. Janet, the girl in the next bed, took advantage of my fear and asked me to consider becoming a Christian. I replied very naively that I thought I was a believer, since I was born in England. Janet more or less borrowed Dr. Billy Graham's words: "If you were born in a garage, would that make you a car?" She then led me thoroughly, totally, irrevocably, to Christ.

Janet was a great role model in my life, and so it's not surprising that some months later at home in Liverpool, when my time came to be sick and admitted to the hospital again, I found myself looking at the situation as an opportunity to minister too. It would have been easy to use the excuse that I was too sick or nervous to bother about anyone else for a while, but with Janet in mind, I looked around and found people just like me, ready to think about life in earnest. I also took some time to think about Jesus and how he never allowed personal weakness to stop him from using the opportunity of the moment. When Jesus was weary and rested at the well, he reached a woman who in turn reached a village for him. When Jesus was chained to weariness, he took the opportunity that weariness gave him to talk to a woman about her soul.

Once when Stuart and I were in Uganda, I got seriously ill the night before we left the country. Standing in the long, hot line to get on the plane, I passed out. I came to on the floor, being held by a young doctor who had been standing in line and had seen me fall. I heard him say, "I think she's having a heart attack." I came around in a hurry as the airline agent called for an ambulance, which rushed me and my worried husband to the emergency clinic a few miles away.

This was a pretty primitive place, but the nurses and the doctor cared for me. I spent a miserable day there. Chained to my sickness, I didn't feel like doing anything except being sick! I could hardly stay conscious to pray, and the thought of putting two sentences together appeared to be quite out of reach.

But Stuart took the opportunities that presented themselves and had a great chance to talk to the young doctor, who told us that he had been trained in Russia. All I wanted was to get out of those "chains" and be on my way, and yet the Lord helped me to pray about this young man. God placed him on my mind and put him in my heart, and what joy there was in telling him about the Lord! We are to take every opportunity to which we find ourselves chained. It takes discipline to think like that—it's a spiritual art.

Paul was literally, not metaphorically, chained to his opportunity. Chained to him with real iron chains, the guards had no option but to listen to the apostle tell them about salvation from sin's chains and death's fetters. I can see the soldiers as they go off duty after a few hours of listening to the apostle expound on a summary of Romans "verse by verse," saying to the next man coming on, "Your turn to be locked up with this crazy man!" Some guards believed in Jesus before their tour of duty ended and went back to Caesar's household to spread the good news around the highest place in the realm.

It is no surprise to see that at the end of the letter Paul sends greetings to the Philippians from the saints "who belong to Caesar's household" (4:22). How did saints get into Caesar's household? We know, don't we? A prisoner called Paul used the opportunity to minister Christ to his guards.

It reminds me of a story that a missionary told me about Ethiopia under Communism. The previous ruling hierarchy had hired Filipino nurses and maids for their children. Most of these women were Christians. The missionaries had done a good job in the Philippines, and now these women found themselves "in Caesar's household" in Ethiopia. They didn't panic when the Communists took over and the royal families they had been serving disappeared. They served their new masters as though they were serving Jesus himself. They just began to minister. They began to be a blessing, and the children of the Communist junta, like the children of the ruling royals before them, began to come to know the Lord. Wonderful!

MINISTRY IN THE PUBLIC SQUARE

Paul saw a golden opportunity to try to get the Romans to allow the rights of Christians to stand in the courts. "I am put here for the defense of the gospel," he says (Philippians 1:16). In other words, Paul declares, "God has put me here in prison to defend our right to preach the gospel." Paul was proud of his Roman citizenship. And he saw it as an opportunity to gain freedom of religion for the church he saw being born in Rome. When he needed to, he used his birth privileges and appealed to Roman justice to give him even more opportunities to minister at the highest levels of government.

Many countries today have a constitution that guarantees freedom of religion. We know some missionaries who took their case to court. They were building their church meetinghouse among the other places of religion in the city, appealing to the law of the land for their right to build an evangelical church building. This was a first. There were no Christian churches at all in that place. Against much opposition and with much prayer, they won their case in the supreme court of the land and opened up the way for other Protestant missions to do the same.

Christians can and should minister at every level of society as good citizens, being a chain of blessing along the way. That's what Paul was doing while chained to the guards in prison. He was preparing for his day in court in order that the gospel could have free reign in the city of Rome.

It is argued that Christians should stay out of politics and not become identified with social issues. Yet, what would the slaves have done without Anthony Ashley Cooper, the seventh Earl of Shaftesbury in England in the nineteenth century, I wonder? He, a committed believer, chained himself to his seat in England's parliament, using his chains as chains of blessing to bring freedom for slaves around the world.

THE MINISTRY OF MODELING

"Because of my chains," says Paul, "most of the brothers in the Lord have been encouraged to speak the word of God more courageously and fearlessly" (Philippians 1:14). Like Paul, we can all minister by the way we respond to what happens to us—which is great, but it is also scary. It means that people are watching us. Some are watching skeptically, and others are hoping we can give them an example to follow when they go through similar trouble.

I don't know about you, but when trouble comes my way, I'm tempted to immediately look around for the people who can support and help me. My first thought is not, "Great! This will give me a chance to tell people about God and encourage other believers who are watching to do the same."

When we came to our church, the elders' wives became my good friends. Within a few years, I watched four of these women pass from this earth to enter heaven. Words are inadequate to express what this did for me. Without exception, what happened to these friends encouraged me in my faith. I did not face death as surely as they were facing death. I observed the secrets they shared together, and those of us who were privileged to be up close and personal said to ourselves, "It's all right to die. Look at how Jesus is helping them." They had hard deaths, but in the end they experienced a glorious "exodus"—and we were helped. They also were very open and shared how the Bible, prayer, and people were helping them. And they were amazingly concerned about *us*! They didn't want to worry us or upset us by sharing too much of the hard information about their illnesses.

In what ways have your responses to what has happened in your life encouraged those who have watched or are watching you? That's a hard question, I know, and I apply it to myself as well.

It's difficult being in a prominent position in a large church when trouble comes visiting—hard for both the parents and the kids. Years ago, one of our children suffered a divorce. We were very conscious that the church was praying, but we were also well aware that the church was watching how we would handle it. Much of it I didn't handle very well, yet the Lord helped me handle some of it with grace, and I know it encouraged other families who were going, or would go, through the same trauma. It also opened doors of ministry I never dreamed possible.

In Philippians 1:19 (Phillips), Paul declares, "For I know that what is happening will be for the good of my own soul." The NIV reads, "For I know that ... what has happened to me will turn out for my deliverance."

It's a spiritual art to allow what happens to us to bring us closer to God and not allow it to drive us further away from him. And it takes the Spirit to help us use the circumstances in our lives for the blessing of others *and for our own soul's growth.*

My immediate response to people who know that something difficult has happened to me is one of withdrawal. I want to hide and keep people out—which isn't always either wise or possible. When someone says, "When are you going to use this circumstance in one of your talks as an illustration of how you began to understand yourself better," I want to shout, "I don't want to use it as an illustration; I just want it to go away!" But I have learned that I can always share how the trouble, whatever it is, has helped me to "know Christ" better.

I was walking with a minister who had just suffered the loss of his only son. A parishioner met us on the way and told the minister how sorry she was. "Will we be hearing about this in church on Sunday, Pastor" she asked. "Not this Sunday," he replied. "But I will *yet* praise God." A good answer.

It takes time to heal enough to minister out of our sorrows. To share with others. When you're not sure how much to share, it's always appropriate to share what you are learning about Christ through the situation. Paul made this an art form, and his troubles and the way he responded to them were a huge encouragement to the church. As the brothers and sisters read about the ways in which Christ ministered to his suffering servant, they were helped to believe that Christ would do the same when their time came, and then they, in turn, would learn to know Christ better.

So Paul tells the church that he is able to rejoice (1:18) because he is helped by knowing Christ in ways he had never known him before the trouble came near to him—and this amazing result makes his chains well worthwhile.

He is also helped by the prayers of the Philippian believers (verse 19). One thing that invariably happens when trouble comes is that Christians around us pray for us. This is no small thing. I have been the recipient of such upholding prayer throughout my life and ministry. What would I have done without it?

One of my greatest joys and privileges over the course of the last years has been to meet with believers in many secret places in lands where Christians are greatly restricted. Talk about encouragement! Who encourages whom? Well, *I* am certainly encouraged. Stuart and I go at their invitation to encourage them, and guess who comes away blessed? To be prayed for by these sweet people is a gift of God that grows your soul in a hurry.

THE MINISTRY OF JOY

As Paul reflects on the preaching of the gospel about Christ, joy floods his heart. In the second half of Philippians 1:18, he declares that he is going to keep on rejoicing, because there is no more appropriate response to God's presence in his life: "I will continue to rejoice, for I know that through your prayers and the help given by the Spirit of Jesus Christ, what has happened to me will turn out for my deliverance" (verses 18b–19).

This is the epistle of joy! The laughing letter of spiritual exuberance. Paul talks about joy that won't quit. He is experiencing laughter of the soul that is a healing balm in itself, and he says it is the result of people's prayers and the work of the Spirit in his life. Do we experience such a thing?

I remember not wanting to go to work one day. But as I readied myself and ate my breakfast, the dark cloud of depression lifted, and I stopped in my tracks to savor the lightness of soul not felt for many a dull day. I knew why. Someone was praying for me! And on top of this, the "help [resources] given by the Spirit" gave me joy.

THE MINISTRY OF COURAGE

Paul knew that he—and we—need courage to keep on going, especially when times get tough. Paul put it this way: "I eagerly expect and hope that I will in no way be ashamed, but will have sufficient courage so that now as always Christ will be exalted in my body, whether by life or death. For to me to live is Christ and to die is gain" (1:20–21).

Being in sticky situations compels us to call on the Spirit of God for help—to give us the courage to continue to confess

Christ against all odds. The beautiful truth is that God gives these resources just when they are needed, and not a moment before.

We had the privilege of knowing Corrie ten Boom, the Dutch woman who helped to rescue Jews in the Netherlands when it was invaded by the Nazis. She told us that when she was a little girl, she heard stories of people who had a choice to confess Christ or to deny him. She became very frightened. She couldn't imagine she would ever be courageous enough to confess Christ if it would mean that she had to lay down her life. She talked to her beloved father about her fears.

The next day, her father walked her to the bus stop as usual so she could go to school. As the bus rounded the corner at the end of the road, her father took the fare out of his pocket. "Corrie," he said.

"Yes, Father?" she replied.

"When do I give you the money for the ride?"

"When I get on the bus, Father," she replied.

"Corrie, if you are ever called to suffer for Jesus, remember that your heavenly Father, like your earthly father, will give you the penny as you get on the bus."

Corrie remembered his words as the Nazis came to take her and her family away to the concentration camps. If you've read her story, you will know that God gave Corrie many pennies—pennies representing the divine provision of courage each time it is needed—for many rather hellish bus rides before she escaped the dreaded death camps.

Don't worry that you won't make a good confession of faith if your life is on the line. That's how you may feel *now*. But *now* is not *then*. God will give you the penny when and if you need it. Paul asked his friends to pray for him in this regard.

WALK WORTHY

Paul sums up his "opportunity" message about ministry with these words: "Whatever happens, conduct yourselves in a manner worthy of the gospel of Christ" (1:27).

My husband, Stuart, tells a wonderful story—purported to be true—of two sons of the king of England. These two young boys—the Duke of Kent and the Prince of Wales—were playing in Hyde Park, and one said to the other, "I bet you sixpence that all fat policemen have bald heads."

"You're on," replied the other. Now they had to find out. At that moment, a little cockney lad walked by, and they offered him sixpence to knock the copper's hat off with a stone. Happy to oblige, the urchin threw a stone and knocked the hat off. The policeman caught them and began to interrogate the young ruffians to find out who they were. He noticed that two of them were dressed very differently from the third. "I'm the Duke of Kent," said the first. "And I'm the Prince of Wales," replied the second.

"Really?" said the copper sarcastically. Turning to the urchin, he said, "And who may you be?"

"Don't worry, lads," whispered the urchin to the king's sons. "I won't let you down." Drawing himself up to his full height and sticking his chest out, he said, "Officer, I'm the Archbishop of Canterbury."

Now why did the policeman and the urchin not believe the king's sons really were who they said they were? Well, we know the answer: it was because the naughty boys weren't walking in a way that was worthy of their calling! Because more is expected of kings' sons, isn't it? As we "conduct [ourselves] in a manner worthy of the gospel of Christ," as Paul exhorts the Philippians, we will behave our belief, so people will believe our words. More is rightly expected of us.

Paul begins his letter by saying, "Paul and Timothy, servants of Christ Jesus." The word translated "servant" can also be translated "slave"—a willing slave, an "eager to do the Master's will" slave. Paul's whole ethos was servanthood. He lived to serve the Lord Christ and the Lord's people. To exercise the spiritual art of ministry wherever he found himself on God's green earth every moment of every day. Would we call ourselves "servants of Christ Jesus"? How are we doing in this exciting adventure of learning the spiritual art of ministry?

QUESTIONS FOR REFLECTION AND DISCUSSION

1. Are you seeing an opportunity in every difficulty, or a difficulty in every opportunity? What happens through you when something happens to you?

2. Paul's letter to the Philippians is an epistle of joy. Make a list based on the following verses, reflecting on the question, "Where does this joy come from?"

   a. 1:3–5
   b. 1:18
   c. 1:18b–21
   d. 2:2–4
   e. 2:17–18
   f. 3:1
   g. 4:4
   h. 4:10

3. Which form of ministry discussed in this chapter spoke to you and why?

 a. ministry in difficulties

 b. the ministry of prayer

 c. the ministry of evangelism

 d. ministry in the public square

 e. the ministry of modeling

 f. the ministry of being drawn closer to Christ

 g. the ministry of joy

 h. the ministry of courage

4. Read Philippians 1:27–30. Make a list of all the things these verses bring to mind for "conducting yourselves in a manner worthy of the gospel of Christ."

5. What does Philippians 1:29 mean?

THOUGHTS FOR PRAYER

Spend some time in prayer:

- for yourself,
- your family,
- your church, and
- for persecuted Christians everywhere.

CHAPTER 2

the spiritual art of
harmony

If you have any encouragement from being united with Christ,
if any comfort from his love, if any fellowship with the Spirit,
if any tenderness and compassion,
then make my joy complete by being like-minded,
having the same love, being one in spirit and purpose.
Philippians 2:1–2

Harmony is concord or agreement. In harmonious relationships, there is no discord. Another word for harmony is "peace"—and making peace is often very hard work. For example, it took a few hundred diplomats to work out a peace agreement in May 1983 to end the conflict between Israel and Lebanon that began in 1982. Then it took thousands of soldiers to enforce and maintain the peace.

The same principle is true for believers: achieving harmony is hard, but being a peacekeeper once a truce is declared is even harder. It's a spiritual art.

The testimony of a community of believers often hangs on the ability of its members to live in harmony with one another and to keep the peace once it is made. Paul appeals to leaders and followers alike to be sensitive to the Spirit's directives and to become ambassadors for unity.

PROMOTING HARMONY AMONG BELIEVERS IS A SPIRITUAL ART

The Spirit's most difficult work in the church is to promote harmony among its members. The art of "keep[ing] the unity of the Spirit through the bond of peace," as Paul puts it in Ephesians 4:3, requires believers who are characterized by humility, persistence, and a passion for the body of Christ. When the Spirit finds someone to cooperate with him in this work, there is rejoicing in heaven, and God smiles. We give him honor when we pursue harmony.

Sadly, other human beings are our biggest obstacles when it comes to practicing the spiritual art of harmony. In fact, sometimes it seems as though the church would be a great place if we could just get rid of the people! As the old saying has it:

> *To live above with the saints we love,*
> *Ah, that is the purest glory.*
> *To live below with the saints we know,*
> *Ah, that is another story!*

But most of us know we can't really do church without people. My husband, Stuart, is fond of saying, "Church isn't somewhere you go; church is something you are."

But how do we do church *with* people? How do we get everyone to love each other? Or even to tolerate one another? How do we bring the Baptist and the Episcopalian together? The Methodist and the Presbyterian? The Lutheran and the Catholic? And how do we achieve harmony beyond the walls of the church in all creeds, classes, and groupings of people? Between Jews and

Arabs, for instance. Between men and women? African-Americans and Caucasians? How do we respect each other's traditions and cultures without reacting defensively and adopting a segregating mind-set instead of an inclusionary one?

Paul knew of only two ways: to ground all relationships in the one relationship all believers have with the Lord Jesus Christ, and to rely on the power of the one Spirit who lives in all believers to maintain unity.

At a convention, a church leader came to me greatly worried. Some of the church's elders had been discussing how to reach out beyond their suburban, white, middle-class neighborhood to the growing Hispanic community burgeoning around them. One of the elders had said, "All well and good, but I don't particularly enjoy being around people who are really different from us." Well, at least he was honest!

If our fellowships are going to be places to which unbelievers want to come, they must know that we would like to have them there—even if they are not like us. We can spend all kinds of time grumbling about these people we don't like showing up at church, or we can realize that they are seekers and that the Lord loves them.

Many churches consciously try to be seeker-friendly by incorporating contemporary music and drama into worship and using different ways to attract young adults and help them feel at home. This is a good thing. We just need to remember that there are also middle-age seekers and old seekers who would be helped to feel at home when hearing a familiar hymn from their childhood perhaps. Rather than allowing music to become a source of serious grumbling and discord in churches (which it often is), we should think in terms of what makes visitors feel welcome—no matter what their age or cultural background is.

Then there are Christians who transfer into our churches. They are "family." There are members of our own extended families we like better than others perhaps, but this doesn't mean we ostracize some members. Some churches try hard to reach out to people of other cultures and invite them to church, but if the visitors sense that people are complaining about the music director or the pastor behind their backs, I can promise you that it will be a brief visit.

Paul writes, "Do everything without complaining and arguing, so that you may become blameless and pure, children of God without fault in a crooked and depraved generation, in which you shine like stars in the universe as you hold out the word of life" (Philippians 2:14–16). In other words, Paul urges, "Don't whine." Christians can and do whine, and if you are a whiner, don't bother trying to share the word of life with unbelievers. They won't listen to you. They have enough whiners in their lives without adding a whole church full of them.

I like the way J. B. Phillips translates this verse: "Do all you have to do without grumbling or arguing." God became frustrated with the children of Israel in the wilderness mainly because they grumbled and argued with him for forty years. Maybe you've experienced a church full of grumblers and arguers, and you are frustrated too.

If you are a parent, you know how it gets to you to have a child who argues every time you ask him or her to do something. My mother would put up with my whining for a little while, and then she would tell me that she could do without such a reluctant helper. "I'd rather do the job myself" she would say. Our daughter-in-law put up a notice in her kitchen that read, "No whining!" It doesn't always stop the whining, but it is a reminder that whiners destroy family harmony. Being cheerful and helpful is a "learned" art. It takes cooperation with the Spirit to get cooperation with others, and we need the Spirit's gentle and cheerful power to help us quit arguing and begin displaying a happy and helpful attitude.

Discord within the body of Christ is a key reason why many people don't go to church. My own father in his early years swore that he'd never again darken the doorway of a church (and he didn't) because a church he had attended split over some disagreement—and his best friend was on the other side of the split. I didn't discover this until I heard about it at his funeral! As a result, my sister and I never darkened the door of a church either. As a follower of Christ, does the fact that our lack of unity drives people away from church bother you? It should. It bothered Paul, and he always tried to be part of the solution.

Unity and harmony among Christians were incredibly important to the apostle Paul. Before landing in jail in Rome, Paul took his life in his hands to travel to Jerusalem despite dire warnings from prophets, church leaders, and disciples along the way. They told him that the Spirit had revealed that he would be killed if he went. Paul had been told the same things by the Spirit. But he was not told not to go, just what would happen if and when he did. Paul went anyway (see Acts 20–21). As predicted, he ended up being nearly torn to pieces by a mob. The Jerusalem church, made up mostly of converted Pharisees who couldn't let go of the rules and regulations of Judaism, was divided in its opinions of Paul—and that's how the whole debacle began. From that point onward, Paul was, as he put it, "in chains for Christ" (Philippians 1:13) until the end of his days.

But personal safety had not been the compass of Paul's life. His compass was the will of God. Having already been through incredible trauma for the sake of the gospel, he put his head down and gave himself not only to evangelism but to "keep[ing] the unity of the Spirit through the bond of peace" in the church (Ephesians

4:3). This is what took him to Jerusalem in the first place (see Acts 20–23).

Are things any better today? Is there harmony in the church? Is there evidence that each person considers others better than himself or herself (see Philippians 2:3)? Are divorced persons welcome in our churches, for example? Single parents? What about lesbians? And if students wander in wearing apparel that shocks us, what happens? What sort of looks do people give them? Do they come back?

Years ago, our church tried to get college students who were far from God to come to church. We managed to get several students from local universities to come to an evening service. After the service, a deacon from our church came to Stuart and said, "We don't want you bringing these kids in here. We don't want them influencing our children." The truth is that the influence would turn out to be for the good!

Stuart insisted that the young renegades were welcome. The deacon then had a swift change of heart and said, "OK, then I'll try to be part of the solution instead of part of the problem. Why don't we start a class called 'Generation Bridge'? We'll take a few of these college students and a few of these church kids and throw them all together with some oldies and study the book of James." The deacon's experiment was a success. Each college student teamed up with an adult, and together they worked through a Bible study on James. At the end of six weeks, they didn't want to stop. It was the beginning of a tide of blessing that has continued to this day. Integration worked, but not without work. That deacon was the key. He committed himself to the spiritual art of harmony for the sake of the community.

What about people of different ethnicities? Do they belong in our local body of believers? Do their children beat a path to our youth groups and attend our summer camps? Do their parents teach our children in Sunday school and sing in our choirs? Do they serve on our church staffs in capacities other than missions? How do they relate to each other? How do they relate to you? If they are in leadership, do we respect them? Do they love one another? Is there a unity and a harmony that make a fractured world gasp as people observe what is happening?

EVERY SHRIMP HAS ITS OWN PUDDLE

Stuart and I recently took part in a church growth convention. I was captivated by the comments of one of the speakers we met there. An expert in worldwide spiritual revival movements, he noted that in the great revivals of history, the Spirit appeared to move in unprecedented ways in certain areas and then moved on. First were the revival movements of the early church in the Holy Land. Eventually, it was Europe that sent out the great missionaries. Then America had its time as a "sending nation." And now it seems that Asia's moment has come, particularly South Korea. "This small nation is leading the charge and sending a tide of blessings in our direction," the speaker noted. "We thank God for them."

He summed up his comments with a vivid analogy. "A movement of the Spirit seems like the ocean," he said. "The tide comes in, and all the shrimps are in the same ocean. Then the tide goes out, and all that is left are puddles. I've noticed that every shrimp has its own puddle!" We all laughed at such a graphic picture.

Is it true of North America? Of Europe? Of other continents? Are there groups of people who seem to be competing in ministry? Did the tide go out? Undoubtedly. And what is left? Isolated puddles with shrimps jumping around in them. Shame on us! And fast on the heels of that thought, I found myself alone with God, asking, "Am I one of those shrimps?" God forbid! May I be known by my efforts to work across the puddles to bring unity and harmony among Christians.

How much does all this matter? Who would want to commit a huge part of one's life to working with the saints when one can work with sinners who are, at times, a whole lot nicer and easier to deal with? Who does it matter to? It matters to God.

When Jesus spoke his last words to the disciples in the upper room, he prayed for them. You can read this prayer in John 17. Many times that night, Jesus prayed for love and unity among his disciples. Then he said, "My prayer is not for [those disciples] alone. I pray also for those who will believe in me through their message, that all of them may be one" (John 17:20–21). That's you and me! Jesus prayed for love and unity among us. Is this prayer being answered in our lives? Wouldn't you like to be the answer to one of Jesus' prayers?

One might have thought that Jesus would have been praying for the world and its salvation that night. Yet Jesus knew that the world would not hear about the great salvation he had left heaven to accomplish if his disciples were using all of their energy to bicker and fight.

UNITY ISN'T UNISON

Unity is not unison. What encourages people here may not encourage people there. But there is a common unity that allows for diversity in the church body. Paul talked much about unity in diversity. "Everyone doesn't need to do things exactly as I do," Paul reminds us. "There is one Spirit but many ways of doing things" (see 1 Corinthians 12:4–11; Ephesians 4:3–13). The unity we have has to do with the things we believe. It takes the Spirit of unity to help us allow for diversity—for welcoming and embracing other people who do things a bit differently from the way we do things.

The problem is that as soon as someone thinks of a different way of doing something, people doing it "the old way" feel threatened. A spirit of competition can spring up, and before you know it, people have taken sides and are criticizing the other group for doing something differently. Oh, to delight in diversity—but a diversity that is unified. Ask God to give you a generous spirit to affirm people who do things a little differently from the way you've always done them before.

"Never act from motives of rivalry or personal vanity," Paul advises, "but in humility think more of each other than you do of yourselves. None of you should think only of his own affairs, but should learn to see things from other people's point of view" (Philippians 2:3–4 Phillips). Harmony happens when everyone works at putting other people first. It is essential for Christian community and for an effective effort in defending the gospel (see 1:27).

So unity isn't unison. Unison is actually easier to achieve than unity, which requires hard spiritual work.

AM I A "PEACE AT ANY PRICE" PERSON?

I would not surrender my principles in order to achieve peace, but I would be willing to pay a personal price to bring about unity in the body of Christ. That is part of what it means to be a "peace at any price" person.

Unity and harmony among believers were foremost on Paul's mind, in his prayers, and on his agenda. Paul worked just as hard at the spiritual art of bringing such unity and harmony in the church as he did at preaching the gospel where it had not yet been heard. He was a "peace at any price" kind of person.

Are unity and harmony foremost on *our* minds? Or do we run a mile at the first hint of trouble? Are we "peace at any price" persons, or are we belligerent fighters who take pride in causing rifts and divisions ourselves?

Paul encountered complaints and arguments throughout the fledgling churches he ministered to. And not just between Jew and Gentile. There were fights between Gentile and Gentile. Even in his beloved Philippian church, Paul discovered trouble between disciple and disciple, leading woman and leading woman.

Euodia and Syntyche, two strong, prominent women in leadership positions in the church — both of whom had worked side by side with Paul — had squabbled with each other (see Philippians 4:2). Does this sound familiar? I wonder if these women's nicknames were "Odious" and "Soon Touchy"? I'm sure they were wonderful women, but when wonderful women get into fights, they can become odious and touchy. I know — I am one!

These women had worked alongside Paul in kingdom work. They were dear fellow workers. Paul, the elderly father figure, could not stand it when his "children" had a falling-out. If you have kids, you know how it gets to you if your own children fight and don't make up. We desperately want our children to live in harmony and unity, even when they're grown. So does God.

I would love to ask Paul, "How do you play peacemaker and counselor, and how do you help mend fractured relationships?" "It's an art," Paul would tell us, "a spiritual art." It takes practice to become a skilled peacemaker or peacekeeper, and it takes the Spirit of unity and harmony himself, working through his people, to mend fences and to turn enemies into friends. But the Spirit doesn't do it on his own. He chooses to work through the very people who can cause trouble themselves. Transformed people. Christian people. Ordinary people such as you and me. Even people who are "peace at any price" people realize that peace in the end is "made" and doesn't just happen on its own, and they can choose to surrender to being part of the solution instead of part of the problem.

A MINISTRY OF ENCOURAGEMENT

So how does God work through people? Paul gives us a hint in the opening verses of Philippians 2. Before he pleads for unity, he appeals to his friends to remember what they have been given in Christ—the experience of Christ's encouragement and his love— and how Paul has taken up this precious ministry of encourage- ment and consolation among them.

> Is there any encouragement from belonging to Christ? Any
> comfort from his love? Any fellowship together in the Spirit?
> Are your hearts tender and sympathetic? Then make me truly
> happy by agreeing wholeheartedly with each other, loving one
> another, and working together with one heart and purpose.
>
> *Philippians 2:1–2 NLT*

A ministry of encouragement includes encouraging Christians to encourage others. What do we encourage others to do? Among other things, get along together! It isn't a matter of unison— everyone agreeing on everything, but a unity that respects diver- sity and celebrates the differences in the body. Being of one mind in the fellowship. I love this definition of fellowship: "two fellows in a ship." When the ship goes up, they both go up; when the ship goes down, they both go down. There is a unique way those in the same boat can help each other out when trouble arises.

Once when I was in Russia, a former prisoner—now an evangelist—gave me a letter written by Christian prisoners there and asked me to take it to Christian prisoners in a United States prison I was scheduled to visit after I returned home. I put the letter in my Bible and took it with me. I read it in all my chapel talks, and as I went from cell to cell, I can't tell you how many tears flowed. Despite vast differences in color, culture, language, and experience, the prisoners understood what each other needed more than I ever could. They were fellows in the same ship—they were in the same boat.

Every Member of the Body Must Practice This Art

The art of encouraging others to love each other is not just for apostles and leaders; it is for all of us.

There are professional counselors we turn to when we have problems, but we must be careful not to make the mistake of thinking we can refer problem people to the professionals and absolve ourselves of all responsibility for peacemaking. We must resist the temptation to shrug our shoulders and leave it to the gifted "loyal yokefellow" (Philippians 4:3) to sort people out. "After all," we may think, "isn't that what we pay the pastoral counselor, the women's ministry person, or the pastoral staff member to do?"

But peacemaking isn't to be left to a paid church staff member. It's a gift. It's an art. And all Christians should be working at it. We have within us the Counselor—the Holy Spirit. He is wisdom itself, and we have in him all we need of skill and discernment. Of course, some will be better at it than others, but all of us are responsible for the relationships within our reach.

Other issues Paul addresses in this passage are humility and self-sacrifice. Paul shows that unity of spirit flows from a willingness to restrain one's own desires in order to satisfy the desires of others. Paul's work as a leader in the church involves dealing with the variety of difficulties that arise when people who come to the church from diverse religious backgrounds and cultures live and worship together. And challenges to unity are bound to arise from such an experiment.

My job as a layperson is to do peacekeeping at my own level. If I work on the relationships that are within reach, I can "put Paul out of business" so he can focus on preaching and teaching. Paul himself had had a ministry of encouragement and consolation among them, and they now needed to do the same for each other.

Keeping One Step Ahead

So how do you give people encouragement? Not by arguing with them! Instead, you lead by staying ahead of them in your spiritual growth and by sharing the lessons you learn along the way. This ministry of encouragement—one of the most important of all ministries in the church—seeks to provide a word in the power of the Spirit, perhaps a word of exhortation from someone strong in faith or a word of counsel to help another gain moral strength from one who is strong in Christ.

I am supposed to be strong in my faith. I am supposed to know my Bible and therefore be able to encourage others to be strong in their faith. Yet, don't forget that people who are strong Christians need encouragement too. I have had people say to me, "I don't pray much for you and Stuart because you are such strong believers." Woe to us! We won't be strong for long if we are unprayed for.

Leaders often need to be encouraged even more than followers. And any follower can learn to be an encourager. I have been encouraged by folks who are just a year old in Christ or by people who cannot read and write but who know God at the deepest level. I have taken heart when a shy woman has slipped a sweet note of appreciation into my hand at the end of a meeting when I thought I had done the worst possible job. Then there is the grandchild who has encouraged me and a grandfather in a wheelchair who has shown me how to suffer with grace and patience and who spends his time encouraging fellow sufferers. Be encouraged to be an encourager. It's a spiritual art that everyone can learn. And mostly you learn by practicing it. Ask yourself these questions: Am I an encourager? Or do I just sit around waiting for someone to show up and encourage me?

I remember visiting a family new to our church. We walked into the living room and found three rather uncomfortable teenagers lined up on the couch, with Mother and Father and Grandma perched around the room. "Let's get down to business," the man of the house said briskly. "We visited your church and liked it. So that's why we asked you to come and talk to us and answer some of our questions. So, Pastor Briscoe, what has your church got to offer my family?"

Stuart was quiet for a moment and then responded, "There's a question I'd like you to answer first. What has your family got to offer our church?"

As far as I remember, they didn't join. People want a church that will "meet their needs." They ask, "What's in it for us?" and not, "What's in us for them?" They are not interested in meeting other people's needs; they're only interested in *their* needs being met. "After all," they reckon, "that's what a church is there for, isn't it?" If they do join but don't find their needs being met, they try another church down the street. For many today, it's all about church hopping and church shopping. If, however, the family comes with a mind to minister—to learn at the very least the spiritual art of encouraging others in the fellowship—strangely they find themselves forgetting their own needs and being a blessing. If they stop to think about it, they discover that their own needs are being met after all.

All of us can do this. You just need to learn to keep one step ahead of the person you are trying to encourage. Keep one step ahead in Bible knowledge, for example. Get to know your Bible so well that you can give people a word straight from Genesis to Revelation to lift their spirits.

Give a Book, Write a Letter, Make a Phone Call

Another way you can begin to practice this art is to ask yourself, "How has God encouraged me?" He has encouraged me through books, for example. I remember being very much alone among my friends after becoming a Christian as a student. The girl who led me to Christ gave me about ten books to read in a month. Then she would meet with me to discuss them.

Among her choice gifts were missionary biographies. It was then that Amy Carmichael walked off the pages of a book and into my life. When I felt alone, I thought of Amy in India, taking on the forces of hell as she rescued little children in the temples from a fate worse than death. At the beginning she was alone. I was fascinated with her story and how she built a fellowship of workers. She writes about the rule of love among those missionaries of the Dohnavur Fellowship in India, and how they worked hard at the spiritual art of unity.

And there was C. T. Studd—a Cambridge graduate, brilliant cricketer, and wealthy Englishman—who gave his inheritance to charity and took off to China to tell others about Christ. Carmichael and Studd are people I could meet only in books, and yet their stories encouraged me to keep the faith and press on, even when I felt lonely and afraid. So if you can't go personally, give a book.

Later on, when I was established in a church, God encouraged me through friends—good friends who encouraged me, just as Timothy, Luke, and Epaphroditus encouraged Paul. Friends who would show up at all times of the day or night. People who would come to my "cell" and sit with me and just give me a word of love.

When you want to encourage someone, think of the way a friend brought encouragement or healing in a relationship you were dealing with. How did they do it? What did they suggest? What helped you? Did they call you, email you, take you out for coffee? Make a list, and then go and do it for someone else.

Ask yourself in a quiet moment, "Whom have I encouraged this week? Whose hand have I strengthened?" Go to the deep place, and sit on the steps of your soul and talk to the Lord; then come back to the shallow places of life and tell those you meet what God said to encourage you, which may then serve to encourage them.

Ask God for an idea of how to solve a particular conflict between people. Better yet, take the discouraged one with you to the deep place where communion with the Lord takes place and sit on the steps together. Wait there until the Prince of Peace joins you, and tell him the problem. Spend time listening for the answer. Read the Scriptures. Look for direction—a warning to heed, a command to obey, a promise to claim. Let the Lord first encourage you, so you can begin to practice the wonderful art of encouraging others.

One thing I have learned to do more than anything else is to ask people, "Will you pray with me?" So often we pray "at" people instead of "with" them. So I've learned to pray first, and then I say (still with my eyes closed), "Now you pray." There is sometimes a startled reaction, but usually—sometimes hesitantly, especially if they've never prayed aloud or with anyone—they pray. This is the best way to encourage anyone—to throw them in at the deep end, but take the chance and watch them swim. God can encourage them better than any person in the world, so take them to him in prayer and leave them there long enough to enjoy his encouragement. Then they themselves can go home and know how to turn to the world's greatest encourager when they need him.

Remember, a ministry of encouragement isn't primarily authoritative and preachy. It isn't bossy. It isn't like giving a lecture. It is the heart of one Christian reaching out to another. Don't start by saying, "The Lord told me to tell you off or put you down," but rather, "The Lord told me to build you up, to encourage you—to put courage back into you so you don't lose heart."

How did the church encourage the apostle Paul? Finding himself discouraged in prison, Paul was encouraged by the church's tangible help in the shape of a gift of money (see Philippians 4:14–18). Maybe it's another way you can encourage someone—a practical way to practice this spiritual art. Being an encourager comes back to you in blessing. Paul the encourager was encouraged by the very ones he encouraged! And this has been my experience as well.

A MINISTRY OF CONSOLATION

Encouragement and consolation go hand in hand. Paul also practiced the spiritual art of consolation, which was based on Paul's experience of Christ's consoling love. "Therefore if there is any encouragement in Christ, if there is any consolation of love ... " (Philippians 2:1 NASB).

The word "console" means "to speak to someone by coming close to his or her side"—and always in a friendly way—not sneaking up on someone you think needs straightening out and hitting them with a spiritual two-by-four. So how do we console people in trouble—people in our orbit who have lost their jobs, their health, or their children to drugs or divorce? Or people in a disaster zone who have lost everything? Maybe it's a new widow who feels that half of her has just gone to heaven, or a mother who knows that her child is in trouble but can't figure out how to help her. Perhaps a relative has moved in and is draining you dry.

First, if we are to bring consolation, we need to physically put ourselves into the situation. By coming close to someone's side, we speak volumes. I call this having "a ministry of presence." The art of putting yourself into another's pain is learned by practice, doing it over and over again, as every other art is learned.

Paul talks about this. He writes, "I am confident in the Lord that I myself will come soon" (2:24). Paul did not make a habit of getting out of prison and hightailing it out of harm's way as soon as the prison doors shut behind him. He says, "I'm confident that I'll come to you soon"; he doesn't say, "I'll get to a safe place and regroup—maybe take some time off and then see about a phone call or a text message." And he doesn't suggest that God send someone else, like Moses did when God told him he was sending him back to Egypt to rescue the Israelites and he responded, "Here am I, send Aaron!" (Exodus 4:13, my translation). A ministry of consolation is really very simple. You just go!

I have served on the board of World Relief for well over twenty years. Every time I go into a refugee receiving center, a war zone, or an AIDS clinic I hear the same thing. Two little words: "You came!" It is an incredible experience to see a person's eyes light up and to hear him or her, either verbally or in body language, say,

"You came to me! You made the journey. When I needed clothes, you came and clothed me; when I was in prison, you visited me."

It's easy to send food, medicine, and clothing. It can simply be an opportunity to clean out our closets. But to have "a ministry of presence" costs us something, and the recipients know it. It consoles them. Paul would not think of leaving prison and saying, "Well, I've done my share of visiting these groups of people and getting thrown in the brig for my trouble. I'll just stay in touch long distance—it's safer." Not Paul.

What about us? Is personal safety the first thing we think of? A ministry of presence is a ministry of consolation, and you don't need a master's in theology to have this ministry. You just need a heart of love and concern for people. One like Paul's. One that is Christ-centered. One that is other-centered.

But how do you know if you are Christ-centered or self-centered? One way I've found out is to gauge my reaction when interruptions occur on a day-to-day basis. People put themselves onto my calendar, and they don't ask my permission to do so! I know at once if I am people-oriented or task-oriented by my reaction to this intrusive behavior. I need to submit my heart to God and spend some time asking him, "What does the consolation of love feel like? How does consoling love behave? Have I even begun to know? And where do I start?"

We can start by asking, "How has God consoled me?" Sit still and think of how God has directly consoled or comforted you. Was it a psalm? A story in the Bible that mirrored your situation and gave you help or instruction? Perhaps God sent a word through the mouth of an Epaphroditus or Timothy; they certainly had a ministry of presence in Paul's life. It may be that God himself made you aware that he had drawn near to give you "the peace of God, which transcends all understanding"—the peace that Paul talks about in Philippians 4:7. Did he hold you together when your world fell apart? Maybe it was the help that God gave you in the form of worship music at just the right moment, assuring you that his consolation was yours for the taking. All of these things are means of consolation.

Remember that Paul is talking about these ministries against the backdrop of trouble between individuals in the church. Often people are hard to live with because they are insecure or have been wounded or abused. To dispense help and comfort, working at the art of understanding and sympathy by lending a listening ear, can only help to mend wounds and foster forgiveness. Just go! God will tell you how to console when you get there.

All of Us Can Cry

In our ministry of consolation, we allow the trouble that troubles others to trouble us. "I have enough of my own troubles, thank you," I can hear you say. Strangely, to cry for others dries your own tears. We are instructed from God's Word "to weep with those who weep" (Romans 12:15 NASB). Paul talks about his ministry among the Philippians as one he carries out with tears in his eyes: "For, as I have often told you before and now say again even with tears, many live as enemies of the cross of Christ" (Philippians 3:18). Paul is weeping for the lost. In the book of Acts, he says, "I served the Lord with great humility and with tears," and, "Remember that for three years I never stopped warning each of you night and day with tears" (Acts 20:19, 31).

Paul wept when he foresaw "wolves" getting into the flock (see Acts 20:29). He wept for the lost; he wept for the saved. He cared deeply with the love of Christ for *people*. Paul learned the art of allowing his tears to talk, his emotions to show, and his feelings to be transparent. Do we? Can we be that vulnerable?

C. S. Lewis said, "Love anything, and your heart will certainly be wrung and possibly be broken."* This is true, but would you rather have a safe but hard heart? Having appealed to the Philippians about the ministries of encouragement and consolation, reminding them of his love, Paul becomes strong in his directives. He tells them that the destructive attitudes they have been exhibiting must stop. "Don't be conceited. Never act for selfish ends," he says. "Avoid a party spirit generated by selfish ambition. Have no part in a rivalry that disrupts unity" (Philippians 2:3, my translation).

Paul exercised a ministry of presence, consolation, and tears. He wanted the church to have the same love for each other that Christ has for the church—showing a self-sacrificial, forgiving grace. To the Philippians and to us today, Paul says, "If in any way you have experienced the tenderness and compassion of God in Christ, be tender and compassionate to each other—not critical and unkind. Give each other the benefit of the doubt." This, Paul assured the Philippians, would give him true joy and make his day (see 2:1–2, my translation).

---

*C. S. Lewis, *The Four Loves* (New York: Harcourt Brace Jovanovich, 1960), 169.

QUESTIONS FOR REFLECTION
AND DISCUSSION

1. Read Philippians 2:1–4. What spiritual arts do you see expressed in these verses?

2. Which section of this chapter touched you or challenged you? Why?

3. Is unity possible if each person is out for himself or herself, if each is seeking his or her own advantage? Why or why not?

4. Are you a person who will fight to prove that your ideas are right? Even if you are right, can you let a point of contention go for the sake of reconciliation and unity?

5. Discuss the ways you have been encouraged or consoled. Share ideas.

6. Read Job 2:11–13. Job's friends came to console him and did a few things right before they did a lot of things wrong. What did they do right in this incident? Discuss.

THOUGHTS FOR PRAYER

1. Pray about the various kinds of attitudes among your fellow church members.

2. Pray about ways to develop the spiritual art of harmony.

CHAPTER 3

the spiritual art of
humility

Never act from motives of rivalry or personal vanity,
but in humility think more of each other than you do of yourselves.
None of you should think only of his own affairs,
but each should learn to see things
from other people's point of view.

Philippians 2:3 (Phillips)

The dictionary definition of "humility" is "an absence of pride; self-abasement," or "the state or quality of being humble of mind or spirit." The spiritual art of humility—of having a modest and respectful attitude toward others—is one of the least practiced of the spiritual arts. Maybe it's because some of us think that being humble means we will be humiliated. "We need affirmation, not defamation," we say to ourselves, and if our self-image has taken a beating, we need building up, not tearing down. But humility has nothing to do with humiliation. It has to do with our view of who God is, not of who we are. It helps us see what God thinks of us, not what others think of us or even what view we have of ourselves. When we practice the spiritual art of humility, we actually come closer to God, who affirms us, loves us, and encourages us. As we humble ourselves under God's mighty hand, he will lift us up (see 1 Peter 5:6; James 4:10), not tear us down. Like all the spiritual arts, being humble takes work on our part, and therein lies the problem.

WORKING AT BEING HUMBLE

Who wants to work at being humble? Not me! My sinful self scoffs at the thought that this art would be necessary for me. Maybe in Mabel's case, or in Tom's, Dick's, or Harry's case! And what's so good about being humble? If you go around being humble all over the place, you'll get trampled underfoot. Don't you need to stand up for yourself?

In our society, we promote ourselves and speak up for ourselves and fight for positions of prominence. We climb the corporate ladder, not caring if we are crushing the fingers of the man or woman on the rungs underneath us. The concepts of promoting others, looking out for others, and helping others before helping ourselves are foreign concepts. We need an example.

"Jesus!" says Paul. "Look at Jesus. There's your example." Jesus provides a portrait of humility that takes our breath away—a picture of the Lord Jesus Christ, who humbled himself so greatly he came from highest heaven to lowest hell. So we have the example of Jesus to follow; the Spirit of Jesus living in us to make it possible to be like Jesus, and the words of Paul to encourage us to let the mind of Christ dominate our attitudes and actions, whatever the cost.

Humility is pure spiritual art. And for this you need the mind of Christ. But the Bible assures us that we have the mind of Christ if we have been born again of the Spirit of God. Christ lived out his life in humility. It was the attitude out of which all of his actions flowed. Humility is not self-disparagement but a sweet un-self-consciousness inspired by the example of the Lord Jesus. "Let this mind be in you," says Paul, "which was also in Christ Jesus" (Philippians 2:5 KJV).

So how do naturally proud people manage to refrain from thinking of themselves more highly than they ought to think? To keep themselves in perspective? It goes against our self-centered nature to consider other people better than we are. And turning the other cheek when everyone else is taking a swipe at our chin isn't easy. Such behaviors aren't natural—but they are spiritual. They are part of the learned art of humility.

In Paul's world, humility was not considered a virtue. Although Jews understood humility as part of their relationship to a holy God, Gentiles considered humility unnecessary at best and stupid at worst. That's why a humble person attracted attention and made onlookers curious. Even though the culture disparaged the idea of humility, when people saw it, they admired and liked it. Think about it. Who is attracted to a full-of-himself person? Who wants to sit next to a self-centered boor who can't stop talking about herself?

Humility that dominates our thinking and motivates our actions is an attractive thing. It is actually a good experience to be with someone who isn't blowing his or her own trumpet and who listens to you with obvious enjoyment instead of dominating the conversation and insisting on being center stage.

When you know that someone is watching you and giving you their full attention, saying by their body language that "you are center stage in my thinking," you warm to that person and find yourself desiring their company. People are looking for someone to be interested in them. Really interested. The hymn in Philippians 2 invites our lives to sing along with the concepts of thinking about others first and foremost, dying to a selfish orientation, and committing ourselves to a sacrificial lifestyle.

WANT TO BE GREAT?
LEARN TO BE SMALL

Many think Paul's description of Christ in Philippians 2:6–11 was used as a hymn by groups of early believers. It begins with attitude. With a mind-set. After all, our actions flow out of our attitudes.

"Your attitude should be the same as that of Christ Jesus," writes Paul, "who being in very nature [essence] God, did not consider equality with God something to be grasped [grabbed—clutched or hung on to] but made himself nothing" (2:5–7a). Think about it. Jesus let go of all that we in our society hang on to, of everything we grab for—status, position, respect. He gave up his rights to be respected, waited on, and adored.

Jesus was known in "Glory Town." When he walked the golden streets, the cherubim and seraphim fell on their faces in front of him, and ten thousand times ten thousand angels sang a song that shook the farthest stars in space. He let all that go. Status, honor, praise, and glory. Paul said that by doing this, Jesus did something great. He humbled himself and became small. "Do you want to be big?" asks God. "Then learn to be small."

After visiting a church to hear a new preacher in town, President Abraham Lincoln is reported to have said of the sermon, "It was good, but he didn't ask me to do anything great." Abraham Lincoln wanted to be challenged. He wanted something to reach for. And that's what God asks of us. God wants us to do something great for him—to be like Jesus, which, paradoxically, means learning to be small. To "let this mind be in you, which was also in Christ Jesus." We need to be like Jesus and release the need for acclaim, affirmation, and a good reputation—and stop allowing what others think of us to chart our course. We must not grab glory or honor that may even rightly belong to us—but rather, with God's help, we can let it go.

So what does this look like? If people put you on a pedestal, you can try falling off. You can learn the art of this sort of honesty—not exhibiting a false modesty but seeking a true assessment of your gifts and talents and keeping them always in perspective. If people put you up there, you can always ask them not to. Don't be afraid to fall off your pedestal. Dress for success—spiritual success. Clothe yourself in modesty.

My mother taught me to dress "properly." In English terms, this meant wearing the right clothes for the right occasion. For example, it wasn't "good taste" to wear casual clothes for a formal event. So my mother, sister, and I would shop with this key principle in mind. It was great fun. We would go to Liverpool (the nearest town) and shop all day. Then we would come home, make a pot of tea, and try everything on, parading up and down the living room in front of each other. Then we'd take time to press our new clothes and hang them up in their proper place.

When the right time and place came, we would dress carefully and present ourselves to Mother, who would tweak our outfits and say, "Now then, you look beautiful. Go out and forget yourselves." Forget ourselves? Yes! Having dressed appropriately, we could get on with thinking about things a lot more important than how we looked in our new stuff. When you clothe yourself with humility before you go out into your day, you not only look good; you are free to think of others rather than being super-self-conscious, which actually is quite obnoxious to other people.

What did Jesus do? Just as he clothed himself in simple, home-made, humble clothing made in Galilee, he clothed himself with humility of spirit. He dressed for success in God's eyes. He also chose to live in humble circumstances—and we can do that too.

"Are you saying we should sell our house and live in a cowshed, Jill?" No, but we can give more than a passing thought to the accumulation of goods and houses and lands in light of our commitment to Christ and his cause. We can also find some humble service to engage in right where we live. Build a house for the homeless, or serve in your community's shelter for battered women. Play with their children. Get in the ditch with the "Samaritan" who has been robbed and abused. Having dressed our spirits appropriately, we will find that we are becoming "other-oriented," seeing people we once ignored as they sat in the ditch while we made our way to our Bible studies at church. We will get off our high horse and into the ditch, with no one around to watch us and applaud, admiring our appearance and envying our robes. To do so would be another way of practicing the spiritual art of humility. In essence, Paul's message is this: "Don't be obsessed with getting your own advantage. Forget yourself long enough to lend a helping hand." Jesus came to lend us a helping hand.

Is there anyone around you who needs a helping hand? Even in suburbia, there is need. Our church is outside the city limits; the inner city is not right at our doorstep. But there is another sort of poverty around us. Broken marriages and families abound. Many of our grandchildren have few friends whose families are intact.

During a Christmas service I once attended, I was sharing my hymnbook with a young woman next to me. Suddenly she sat down. She wasn't feeling well, so I helped her out and took her to a place to recover. I listened to her story. She was a single parent who was working two jobs so she could keep her kids. But she wasn't making enough money to feed them and care for them properly. She had fainted, literally, for lack of food. I asked her if she had Christmas presents for the kids. She burst into tears. "Yes," she replied. I discovered that she had donated plasma to earn money to buy the gifts.

Now this is a respectable suburban church setting. We are amazed how many people use our food pantry and clothes closet, how many have no money for rent or medicine, how many need help to find jobs, how many need a friend.

When you are self-absorbed, you don't notice the person you share your hymnbook with. When you are thinking about the needs of others, a whole new world opens up.

LEARN TO LAUGH AT YOURSELF

As we learn the art of humility, it's important that we don't take ourselves too seriously. Once we start listening to our own press, thinking that we are really very important people, humility tip-toes out the door. Learn to laugh at yourself—a lot! The Bible tells us to humble *ourselves* and not wait for someone else—like God!—to do it for us. "Humble yourselves," says the Bible (James 4:10; 1 Peter 5:6), or God will humble you (see Daniel 4:37; Matthew 23:12). Take responsibility to practice this spiritual art.

As Paul begins to paint this wonderful word portrait of Jesus in Philippians 2, he says that Jesus "made himself of no reputation" (verse 7 KJV). Think about that. Our reputation, what people think about us or say about us, is very important to us—too important sometimes.

Years ago, I was working for a youth mission in the United Kingdom. We were reaching many young people who hung around the pubs at night. Some came to Christ as a result of our outreach. One day, Trevor, a young man who was a relatively new believer, came to our house to ask if I would go to one of the pubs and talk to his friends about the Lord. "They're really interested, Jill," he said, "but I can't answer all their questions. So I told them I knew someone who could. Would you come with me tonight?"

I was surprised at my response to this young man. I didn't want to go. Reluctantly, I said I would, hoping he wouldn't notice my hesitancy. When he had gone, I spent time with the Lord talking it through.

"Why don't I want to go?" I dared to ask God.

"You're afraid of your reputation," he answered.

"Oh, yes," I replied, "I suppose I am. What if someone sees me going into the pub and tells someone about it? What would they think of me? What would they think of you? They know I'm a Christian who works at the youth center, and I may not be able to explain why I'm going into such a place."

Yes, I decided that the Lord was right. I was indeed concerned about my reputation.

That night I read Philippians, asking that some principle I found in the letter would show me how to answer my young friend. Of course, when I came to Philippians 2:7, I stopped in amazement. There was my answer: Jesus "made himself of no reputation." "Well, now," I said to myself, "what was I worried about *my* reputation for? He didn't worry about his." I had a choice to make. I could make myself of no reputation for Jesus; or I could play it safe, stay home, and let someone else put his or her reputation on the line and answer the questions. Anyway, why couldn't these kids come to church and get their questions answered if they really wanted to know? Why bother me? As I tuned in to my thoughts, I was ashamed of myself. Soon I was on my knees, the question settled.

I went into the pub with Trevor and met his wonderful friends. That act of obedience started a movement of the Holy Spirit across the town. Jesus didn't hang on to his reputation, and he didn't care about recognition for who he was. The NIV puts it this way: Christ Jesus "made himself nothing." He came to a pub—in fact, he was born in the stable that belonged to the pub!

GOD'S SONBEAM

What's more, Jesus emptied himself, not of his deity, but of his glory—"the glory," Jesus said in John 17:5, "I had with [the Father] before the world began." Then Jesus came to earth's little space to save us.

What is glory? The Bible talks about the "radiance of God's glory" (Hebrews 1:3)—in other words, the brightness, the outshining beam, of the Father's glory.

The sun's rays diffuse light and heat, testifying to God's benevolence. The earth is blessed by this gift of goodness and brings forth life in the form of plants and trees. We could not exist at all, were it not for the sun's rays. And through the Son of God, the Father displayed his glory and dispensed his benevolent grace to the whole universe. Jesus is just as much sun as the sunbeam. Jesus is God's ray—God's "Sonbeam." The Son "rayed" forth the splendor of the Father.

When I was a kindergarten teacher, I loved to watch the children paint and color. Five-year-olds always drew the sun with spikes sticking out of a yellow ball. "What are these?" I asked them. "The sunbeams," they answered. We know they were right. The sun spews out rays of light, and to the naked eye they look like spikes sticking out of a yellow ball. We know the sunbeams are just the same essence as the sun itself. So it is with Jesus. He was God's Sonbeam—made of the same essence: "Who, being in very nature God ...," the Bible wonderingly tells us in Philippians 2:6.

As I thought about this concept years ago, a poem was birthed in me:

It started with a sunbeam
Bound for a crossbeam,
A Sunbeam from the Glory
Shining on the earth.
Beloved of the Father,
Begotten not created,
Infinitely precious,
Borrowing my birth.

Born a little boy beam
Bound for a crossbeam,
Favorite of the Father
Takes a servant's place
Stripping off His royalty,
Robed in humanity,
Smile of His Father
With tears on His face.

Birthed in obscurity,
Living in poverty,
King as a commoner,
Revealing God to men.
Carrying my cross for me
All the way to Calvary
Sonbeam a'dying—
Then shining again!

> *Shine in my darkest days,*
> *Teach me to live in praise;*
> *Deal with my doubting*
> *And use all my pain.*
> *Mirrored in my mendedness,*
> *Helping all my helplessness,*
> *Sonbeam of my Father,*
> *Light up my life again!*

Jesus, God's Sonbeam, though of the same essence as God, though equal with God, let the glory go and became a man. He didn't give up anything of his deity, but rather added humanity to who he was in the beginning: "being made in human likeness.... being found in appearance as a man [found in fashion as a man (KJV)], he humbled himself" (2:7c–8a). Where did this stupendous humbling happen? In a back alley behind the inn. Down the lane and in a corner. Among the fleas and ticks and animals. He came incognito through the back door of our world to Bethlehem's little town.

Where do *I* go in the alleys of the world? What things do *I* do in secret or give in secret? How many times is my right hand unaware of what my left hand is doing? Do *I* do anything incognito? Jesus gave his glory clothes away, swapping them for swaddling clothes.

STEPPING DOWN OR STEPPING UP?

Do you get the picture? Jesus stepped down. He exercised voluntary humility, "taking the very nature of a servant" (2:7). He looked down, stepped down, came down, and knelt down and washed our feet. He lay down on a cross and went down into hell itself. For Jesus it was all about "down." For us, all too often, it's all about "up." Sadly, many of us in the church want only to serve in an advisory capacity. We want to train others to wash people's feet, but we don't want to wash them ourselves. "We don't do feet," we say.

Jesus was made "a little lower than the angels" (Hebrews 2:9). Think of it—a little lower than the angels and a little higher than the animals! "In human likeness"—disguised as a child, unrecognizable to those in Bethlehem that Christmas night.

The angels from the realms of glory who winged their flight o'er all the earth—those who sang creation's story and proclaimed Messiah's birth—must have been utterly confounded by Jesus' changed status: "found in fashion as a man"; humility wrapped in a blanket, God's supernova, fallen from heaven to a mother's arms, a beautiful Jewish baby, hay in his hair. Or as hymnwriter Charles Wesley put it in the hymn "Let Earth and Heaven Combine": "Our God contracted in a span, / Incomprehensibly made man."

The angels were amazed at Jesus' humbling. Am I? Or do I want to be treated as though I am a little *higher* than the angels? God may well wonder if we aren't acting in a way that's lower than the animals! He's not impressed. "I will humble all who walk in pride," God says (Daniel 4:37, my translation). He despises pride, and he hasn't changed his mind about that. So Jesus Christ laid aside the trappings of his deity—his appearance and his status before the heavenly beings—and came to us. What were these trappings he laid aside? His scepter, connoting his power; his crown, representing his authority; his robes, signifying his majesty and glory; and even his judgment throne. His scepter speaks of his control, and to me, one aspect of the incredible humbling of Jesus was the way he let go of the control that was his and submitted to dependence on a teenage girl and a humble carpenter for his life and livelihood.

The Creator became the created! In Colossians 1:16 (MSG), Paul writes, "For everything, absolutely everything, above and below, visible and invisible, rank after rank of angels—*everything* got started in him and finds its purpose in him"—the one who created the angels who were now singing him to sleep! I wonder if the angels watching Mary wrap the baby Jesus in swaddling clothes might have felt a little insecure?

The year my daughter gave birth to a baby boy, I wrote a Christmas poem that included these lines:

> *God in embryo, growing to birth size,*
> *a baby boy became.*

How helpless a newborn is. Is there anything quite as dependent as a newborn? Jesus voluntarily gave up being in control in order to become dependent.

I know how hard it is for me to give up control. I'm not talking about giving up responsibility, but I have within me this huge desire to control everything—people included. It helps to whisper to my soul, "Let this mind—Christ's mind—be in me."

Jesus had control, and he let it go. He allowed his Father to have the control. He submitted to his Father's will. It was his Father's will that he be born in a manger and die on a cross. It was his Father's will that he was a poor man instead of a rich man. It was his Father's will that he was a nobody in the eyes of the world in order that he might be a somebody in the eyes of God. In surrendering his life and his will to God, Jesus was saying, "Father, you choose."

That's what humility does. It says to God, "*You* choose." Jesus said, "As I live by the Father, so you are to live by me" (John 14:20, my translation). Can you say to God, "You choose. You know best. You control my life, and I will submit my will to you"? Only the humble mind can say that. The prideful mind says, "I choose. I know best. I can run my own life. I can make something of myself. I don't need to settle for obscurity or ignominy."

But Jesus was born in ignominy and died in ignominy. He was no stranger to stigma. Onlookers questioned Mary's purity and the dubious story of Jesus' birth. Jesus descended on that great graph of grace from heaven's heights to the lowest depths for us. If we have the mind of Christ, we can make small graphs of grace for others. We can surrender our pride and forgo our dignity too. So, do you want to be big? Learn to be small.

CONSIDER THE SOURCE

Jesus "humbled himself and became obedient to death—even death on a cross" (Philippians 2:8b). He died for me; I died in him. So I need to ask myself, "Is there evidence of my daily dying to my sinful self? Do people see it? Am I dying to my own self-importance? One way I can find out how well I am doing is to ask, "How do I cope with criticism. Do I welcome it? Or do I criticize those who criticize me?"

The first thing to do when you are criticized is to "consider the source." Some people believe they have the gift of criticism. They even claim to have a ministry of criticism! They don't call it that, of course; they call it a gift of discernment. They think it's a spiritual art. There certainly *is* a spiritual gift of discernment, but it has to do with discerning spirits. We have to be on our guard, though, because the Devil is a critic of Jesus and his people—a slanderer and an accuser (see Revelation 12:10). We have to be careful not to do his work for him.

Leadership invites critics—it goes with the territory. My husband says that a Christian leader needs the mind of a scholar, the heart of a child, and the skin of a rhinoceros. When he heard this, our senior pastor said, "Oh, that's what is the matter with me. I have the heart of a scholar, the skin of a child, and the mind of a rhinoceros!"

Receiving criticism can be a great way to keep us humble. Paul was criticized his entire life. In Philippians, he is criticized for the way he preaches (see 1:17). In 1 Corinthians 4, he talks about being criticized for assuming a position as an apostle. The people didn't believe that God had called him to this, and they wanted to know why he had taken this authority on himself.

Paul responds, "I care very little [it is a very small thing (KJV)] if I am judged by you or by any human court" (1 Corinthians 4:3). Note that Paul doesn't say it means nothing to him to be judged by the world. We should listen carefully to our critics and pray about what they say. We need to own what is true and disown what is not. Paul had learned how to handle critical people—to let it be a "small thing." Learning how to do that is a spiritual art. For most of us, criticism is a "big thing," not a small thing. Paul goes on to say that he doesn't even evaluate himself because, he says, "it is the Lord who judges me." Therefore, judge nothing before the appointed time. Wait until the Lord comes, who will "bring to light what is hidden in darkness and will expose the motives of men's hearts" (4:5).

In essence, Paul says, "I want to know what *God* thinks of all this stuff that people are saying about me. That's the most important thing. He alone knows the motives of my heart. I'm accountable to him." Ah, there it is. He says that he'll leave the judging to God, who one day will judge the "motives of men's hearts." Criticism drove him to God, from whom he got his orders and who evaluated and affirmed him. God encouraged him not to think of himself more highly than he ought to think but not more lowly than he ought to either! He reminded Paul of his call on the road to Damascus—God's call on his life was ultimately all that mattered. God was his Master, and he would answer to him and him alone.

Being criticized can help us to run to God. We need to acknowledge any truth in the accusations and listen to what God thinks about us. It takes humility to listen to both the criticism and to God. But in the end, if you go to the Lord in humility, being willing to hear what he says, you will be lifted up above it all.

I serve as the editor of *Just Between Us*, a magazine for ministry wives and women in leadership. I once received a letter that read, "Who do you think you are, Jill Briscoe? God's gift to pastors' wives?" It put me on my face before God. I owned what I needed to own—perhaps thinking too highly of myself in this regard, and of this I repented; I didn't own the implication, though, that I didn't have a heart for pastors' wives. And God helped me allow the criticism to make me a better encourager of ministry wives.

It's natural that these things cut deeply. But I take every accusation to the Lord and try to stay at his feet long enough to find out if there is any truth in it. I try to look in the Bible for a principle that directs me to know what to do with the criticism. Always I pray that I will be suitably humbled by the experience so that I can become more like Jesus. Try to allow the criticism of others to make you more like Jesus. That's an art—a spiritual art.

Unless you learn this art, you won't be able to give criticism to others. It takes a humble person to be able to give criticism when and where it is due. Start by giving credit where it's due before you give criticism where it's needed. For example, when correcting children, it's best to begin by praising something they're doing right rather than admonishing them for what they're doing wrong. Before offering correction, comment on something that is right and noteworthy about them, which makes them more open to your feedback and more receptive to the rebuke or correction. The same principle applies to adults. Try to find something to affirm first.

When you allow God to keep you humble, he will make you like his Son, who was "gentle and humble in heart" (Matthew 11:29). Paul writes in Philippians 4:5, "Let your gentleness be evident to all." People who need correction are much more likely to respond to gentleness than harshness. To love rather than unlove. To correction rather than rebuke. So try to learn the art of humility, which is of great and lasting value to the body of Christ.

SOMETIMES THE SMALL MEETING IS THE BIG MEETING

I am frequently invited to speak at church gatherings, women's group meetings, and conventions, and even to travel to faraway places as a featured Bible teacher. Years ago, when looking at a pile of invitations, I remember struggling with my motivation to take only the "big" meetings. The important events! After all, when our children were still at home, I limited myself to one overnight event a month and one out-of-state engagement. The rest I filled in with home ministry in my church and area. But I was getting so many invitations that it was tempting to go for the "big" opportunities.

Praying about it one day, I asked God for something I could do to check this tendency. At once I knew what to do. Whenever

I took a "big" opportunity, I would accept a small one. If I spoke to thousands one weekend, I would travel to the middle of a small state to meet with a group of women in a farmhouse the next. And I discovered many things about God, myself, and other people this way.

One of my biggest discoveries was that sometimes the "small" meeting was the "big" meeting. Incredible things were wrought in the lives of a couple of people in a group in the middle of nowhere, which then resulted in reaching thousands. And I got to invest in a circle of people who took me into their hearts at a deep level to become my prayer partners and friends for the journey and who invested in our ministry.

It happened in a place called Boondocks. Yes, it did—there really is such a place. The meeting was in a farmhouse in a corn-field, and a few women met to hear me teach the Bible for a day. At the end of the day, one of the women asked me about our radio program. "What can we do to get it on the radio in our area?" she asked. I told her that we buy radio time, which is terribly expensive, and that we would have to find a station that broadcasts into the area. I was pretty sure there wasn't one near them.

She didn't say anything else, but after I had gone home, she made some calls and found a Christian radio station. She asked how much it would cost to broadcast a half hour of our radio program. He told her. It wasn't cheap. A few weeks later, we received a check to cover the cost for a trial run. We did it. She has supported us ever since. That whole area of the country, which is out of the orbit of the Christian circuit, has been able to listen to Bible study on the radio every day as a result of this "small" opportunity.

These kinds of things seldom happen in a crowd. In the big events. So something I did to keep my pride in check ended up being a blessing to me, giving me "heart partners" in ministry, and bringing the gospel to an area bereft of Christian teaching—thereby blessing others.

We need to die to the nonsense of controlling our own lives and ministry, in fact, our own anything—our own schedule, time, money, status, and the trappings of self-importance. Jesus left *everything* behind him. All his things. Do we have our "things" in perspective? Cultivating a spirit of humility will help us keep ourselves the "right size" in our thinking.

Paul said that we shouldn't allow a spirit of rivalry to cause divisions among us. Rivalry about ministry. Even rivalry about material things. Do we have these things in perspective? What kind of car do we drive? How do we spend our money? Where do we go for our leisure time? Do we easily say no to legitimate pursuits in order to serve people? Are we dead to the lure of our things and alive to the things of Jesus?

Jesus died on the cross. He died to a career—he was only about thirty-three years old when he died. He died to fame and fortune. He insisted that those he healed not tell anyone (see Matthew 8:4, for example). He died to a career as a super-rabbi, spending his days on earth debating in the schools of Hillel and Shammai—prominent religious teachers of the day. He died to companionship among the elite and chose to spend his time with tax collectors and sinners. So Jesus modeled humility for us.

One of the things that will really keep us humble is to spend time with the disenfranchised, the poor, the oppressed, the prisoners, and the outcast. Such experiences as serving with my friend in a maximum security prison, visiting a relief center at a garbage dump in the Philippines, helping displaced people find a toilet or some water to wash themselves, and talking to beggars in Peru have changed my life and humbled me beyond measure. As I learn to wash the feet of suffering people, I cry. How rich and spoiled

I am. How soft. How unworthy to serve these people—to give a cup of cold water to the persecuted or a blanket to the naked. Why should I have the privilege to be fed and warm, well and strong? Why do I live in a country with police protection, a country that is comparatively safe? Why is my stomach full? Why do I have a bed to sleep in and so many clothes in my closet? I am humbled by my wealth. I am humbled by the poverty of many in this country and around the world.

We so often rate and value events, ministry, and even people according to their importance in the eyes of the world. Instead, we need to think about their importance in the eyes of God. In a society that is market driven and filled with "people worshipers," the church needs to be careful that it doesn't allow the world's values to drive ministry.

LET GOD GIVE YOU YOUR THRONE

Having given us a portrait of pure humility to emulate, Paul concludes his picture of Jesus:

> Therefore God exalted him to the highest place
> and gave him the name that is above every name,
> that at the name of Jesus every knee should bow,
> in heaven and on earth and under the earth,
> and every tongue confess that Jesus Christ is Lord,
> to the glory of God the Father.
>
> *Philippians 2:9–11*

After the cross, God essentially declared to the world, "That is what you thought of Jesus; now I will show you what *I* think of him." And God raised Jesus from the dead, highly exalted him, and placed him on the judgment throne. God gave him his throne, his place. God chose it, and God gave it. We must let God exalt us and not try to exalt ourselves. When others put us down, let God put you up, but also let God place you where he wants you in his grand cosmic plan. We do not choose our own place of ministry. He has the very place in mind.

God will take the humble in heart and give them the place of influence he has prepared for them in life and service. We don't need to manipulate or fight our way to that place. We simply need to volunteer to be small, remember that we're dead, and let his resurrection life motivate and empower us to run the race marked out for us. As we are obedient on a daily basis, one day we will find ourselves in the Lord's chosen place of influence. All we need to do is volunteer. Volunteer for what? Humility! That's all. God will do the rest.

Say, "I'll be humble for you, God," and God will say, "Then I will place you where I will." So all we need to do is to volunteer.

JESUS WAS A VOLUNTEER

Jesus volunteered. No one made him jump over heaven's walls. No one bribed him to leave his comfort zone and ask for trouble. No one hired him. He didn't ask what the benefits of the job were—health care, vacations, insurance. The Father didn't say, "How much do I have to pay you to go down there and sort out this unbelievable mess?" No one twisted Jesus' heavenly arm. He came. He volunteered.

I have chosen to live the life of a layperson in the church. I volunteered. For well over thirty years, I put in as many (or more) hours as paid staff members as I built and led a women's ministry that had the privilege of influencing thousands of women. At several points along the way, I was offered a paid position. There was no right or wrong way to respond to this; there was only God's way for me. As I prayed about it, I was clearly led to do the job offered but to do it as a volunteer. It has been a great journey of faith for me. And one thing has happened as a result: I found a way to inspire and challenge thousands of people to do the same. All of us can volunteer to serve Jesus full-time.

Clearly there are times to accept a "professional" post in ministry, but there are times when it does no harm to ask God if he wants you to be a volunteer. When I asked God about the many opportunities that came my way, he told me, "Do this as a member of the body of Christ for me without remuneration." These were my instructions. No one else's—just mine. I obeyed. No one bribed me; no one twisted my arm. I volunteered. And God has provided all that I have needed and more. Let God give you your assignment for him, whether it is a paid position or not. Let God give you your throne. It has been such an adventure that I wouldn't have missed it for the world.

This form of ministry means you depend on God for direction, protection, and affection. You have to spend a lot of time with Jesus alone to get your marching orders each day. No one is going to give you a "to do" list. You get that from your heavenly Father every morning of your life in the deep place where you sit on the steps of your soul and talk to him firsthand. Can you imagine anything more thrilling and fulfilling?

Humility is a spiritual art. It takes practice. So ...

Want to be great?
Then learn to be small,
A lover of Jesus
And servant of all.

Want to be rich?
Then learn to be poor;
Give Him your everything
Then give Him more.

Want to be happy?
Then learn to be sad;
Weep with the weeping,
Visit the bad.

Want to be great?
Then learn to be small,
A lover of Jesus
And servant of all!

QUESTIONS FOR REFLECTION
AND DISCUSSION

1. Read Micah 6:8. List the three things God requires from his servants.

2. Define humility. Put it in your own words.

3. Read the hymn found in Philippians 2:6–11. Try to put it into your own words. Choose a particular phrase and share why it convicts you.

4. Discuss the reasons you think volunteerism has fallen on hard times.

5. How do you help yourself to stay humble?

6. Write down one thing you learned about receiving criticism or giving it.

THOUGHTS FOR PRAYER

1. Pray for the church—that attitudes of humility will be predominant and that God will deal with pride and arrogance.

2. Pray for yourself—that you will learn and practice the spiritual art of humility.

3. Pray for your children and for those you influence.

4. Pray for the people who are watching you—that they will be open to having their own lives examined and transformed as they see you emulating Christ.

CHAPTER 4

the spiritual art of
intimacy

I want to know Christ and the power of his resurrection
and the fellowship of sharing in his sufferings,
becoming like him in his death, and so, somehow,
to attain to the resurrection from the dead.
Philippians 3:10–11

At the end of his life, Paul still wants more. He is fine-tuning his relationship with Christ and settling for nothing less than knowing all that it was possible to know of him at every level of his being. This growing intimacy Paul talks about is the Spirit's art in our lives. Our part is to practice being aware of the presence of God.

Developing an intimate relationship with God is like developing an intimate relationship with a person—your wife or husband, for instance. For example, Stuart and I have been married for forty-nine years. I thought I knew Stuart well before I married him, but it has taken all this time to know him in a deeper way than I ever thought possible. After all these years, most of the time I can tell what he's thinking as we're engaged in conversation with others at a meal, or I can anticipate how he will react in a given situation. I also instinctively know if he is hurt and worried, happy and content. I know how to cheer him up and how to make him sad. It takes time—and hard work—to grow in intimacy like this.

It's an art—it's called marriage. So it is with God. Developing intimacy with God takes time and work as well.

How would you characterize your relationship with God right now? Do you feel isolated and far from God, or do you feel a deep connection and spiritual intimacy? Since you first came to know him, have you experienced a growing knowledge of who he is and how he thinks? Have you discovered how he reacts and what gives him joy and sorrow? Do you know instinctively?

Spiritual intimacy is a learned art. It starts when we come to know God, when we commit our lives to him. Then it is dependent on help from the Spirit of God, who knows Christ and will make him known to us in our joys and in our sorrows. Do we want to know Christ in depth? Do we want to know him more than we know him now? For this we need divine help.

I WANT TO KNOW CHRIST MORE

As we think about knowing Christ more, we must be honest with ourselves. We say the words, but do we mean them? Do we want to know him more, love him more, and please him more? Is it our deep wish to enjoy his presence in ways we have never known before? Go to a spiritual depth we've never experienced? Know a touch of his Spirit that leaves us breathless in worship, vividly aware of him in ways we never believed possible? In other words, are we hungry for more of God?

The strange thing is that we can answer yes to all these questions about wanting more, but many of us would have to admit we've really settled for less. Why? Perhaps because we know that the art of knowing God at a deeper level is a lot of spiritual work and discipline, and our lazy hearts don't want to do it. It could also be we are deliberately lazy because we have a sneaking suspicion that having more of God means God having more of us, and we don't want to surrender any more of ourselves.

God's work is to establish this hunger, this longing, for him in our hearts. "It is God who works in you," Paul declares (Philippians 2:13). Our work is to give him the time of day to satisfy the longing that the Spirit of God creates within us. And this was Paul's desire, even in the closing days of his life. He wouldn't settle for anything less than knowing everything it was possible to know of God here on earth.

Maybe we've been shying away from practicing the spiritual art of intimacy with God — allowing the Spirit to take us to the next level — because we read something like these rather frightening words of Paul from Philippians 3 about how such intimacy is linked with Christ's sufferings. Perhaps we are tempted to object that knowing God in depth shouldn't have to be linked to experiencing hard times. But in the very same sentence, Paul talks about "the fellowship of sharing in [Christ's] sufferings." When we realize that we can get really close to God's heart when we go through life's dark experiences, we back off, saying, "Wait a minute. Why can't I get to know God in the easy times — in the sunshine, in the springtime?" But the truth is, we all know it is under dark skies and in the wintertime that God comes especially near. Spiritual closeness often happens in the university of life's bitter, not better, moments. That's when we get on our knees and dare to whisper, "Whatever means you use to take me to that heart-deep place, Lord, I'm asking you to take me there — because I want to know you more." God will take you at your word, I assure you.

Being in Christ involves fellowship with him at all points — his life, his death, his sufferings, and his glory. Each believer by identifying with him incurs a measure of afflictions. As Paul puts it, "It has been granted to you on behalf of Christ not only to believe on him, but also to suffer for him" (Philippians 1:29). Identifying with Christ in his sufferings is not something that was reserved for believers in Paul's day; it's something all Christians are called to do. For example, in many countries today, converting to Christianity is cause for persecution. Stuart and I have been with Christians who were thrown out of their homes, or worse, for believing in Jesus. Although we don't suffer such drastic consequences in the West, some of our young people are excluded from social events and ridiculed for their faith or churchgoing, their behavior, and even their clean language because they are Christians. Such difficulties can lead the one who is suffering to turn to God for help and encouragement and hence to come to "know Christ" more.

If I want to be like Christ in my living and in my dying, "becoming like him in his death," I need to accept my piece of the action where suffering is concerned. Consider the words of Amy Carmichael, one of my favorite missionaries, who suffered in many ways and who knew great intimacy with God as a result:

> *Hast thou no scar?*
> *No hidden scar on foot, or side, or hand?*
> *I hear thee sung as mighty in the land,*
> *I hear them hail thy bright ascendant star*
> *Hast thou no scar?*
>
> *Hast thou no wound?*
> *Yet I was wounded by the arches spent*
> *Leaned me against a tree to die, and rent*
> *By ravening beasts that compassed me I swooned,*
> *Hast thou no wound?*

> *No wound? No scar?*
> *Yet as the master shall the servant be,*
> *And pierced are the feet that follow me:*
> *But thine are whole: can he have followed far*
> *Who has no wound nor scar?**

As we follow Christ, there will inevitably be wounds and scars. What will we do when we are wounded and hurt? Can we allow the work of the Spirit to take us deeper in our knowledge of God because of the winds of adversity?

Years ago, I received a phone call telling me that one of our children was in dire trouble. It was a total shock. I put the phone down and got on my knees. After some frantic prayers, I started to listen to myself. I was praying like an unbeliever. Angry and hurt, I began to accuse God of being asleep at the switch. I stopped praying (which was just as well), walked to my desk, and opened my journal. I put the dark date at the top of the page and wrote, "Oh, this is going to do wonders for my prayer life!" It did. As I experienced suffering that only a mother can know, I began to hear the voice of God. And so I listened instead of complaining, and I submitted to what he wanted to teach me about himself in the situation.

In the end I was able to whisper a prayer that went something like this: "Show me how to use this trouble to drive me to you and not away from you so I can know you more." God showed me how, and I know him more today than I did before the event.

---

*From Amy Carmichael, *Toward Jerusalem* (Fort Washington, Pa.: CLC Publications, 1988). Used by permission of the publishers.

That day I chose to practice the spiritual art of knowing Christ more in "the fellowship of sharing in his sufferings." Here in these painful times we can learn how to let the suffering take us further in our heart understanding of the Lord and his sufferings instead of turning from him in anger and pulling back from him. Do we use our pain to open the door to spiritual insight and knowledge of the heart of God? Try to "go with the pain" all the way into God's heart. Get down on your knees and use the painful thing that has happened to you to open a dialogue with God. Shape your pain into a prayer, and pray it. Above all, ask God to help you use the pain to understand yourself, Christ, and others better. Put time aside on your calendar to address these painful situations in your life with him. If you don't put it on your schedule, you likely won't get around to doing it.

So how well do we know Christ? Do we want to know him more than we know him now? Is there a hungering and thirsting to find him in another place, in another way, than we've ever experienced him before—even if the pathway leads through the dark door of suffering? Do we allow our troubles to produce a richness in our relationship that is new?

Some think that knowing more of God simply means knowing more about religious rules and regulations and keeping them. They also believe that God will reward their good behavior with some sort of impenetrable shield protecting them against adversity. Before Paul came to know Christ, he was a Pharisee who believed that meticulously keeping the rules would gain God's favor, blessing, and protection. Moreover, he was able to claim that he was blameless as far as the law was concerned (Philippians 3:6). Nobody disputed that. But to know more about the rules doesn't necessarily lead to knowing more of God deep inside or being rewarded with exemption from suffering. It doesn't shield you from trouble. In fact, you can know the rule book by heart, dot all your i's and cross all your t's, and still encounter pain and problems.

Some suffering we undoubtedly bring on ourselves by being disobedient to God, and some trouble comes as a result of others being disobedient to God, but there is also trouble that is simply part and parcel of life lived in a period of time called "after the fall." Trouble comes to all of us on planet Earth, whether we keep the rules or break them, but God offers his children his steadying hand. Head knowledge about why God allows bad things to happen to good people doesn't always help when good people experience some of those bad things. But, you see, God is after our hearts. "Come near to me," he says. "I will draw close to you, and you will *not* be disappointed" (James 4:8, my translation).

THE HEART MUST BE INVOLVED

When you get married, there are rules you need to obey from the heart to keep the relationship intact. Paying mere lip service to each other where fidelity is concerned, for example, will not promote depth in a marriage. The heart must be involved. To be outwardly obedient and faithful but to love your spouse less and less because you are feeding your love for someone else more and more leads to a miserable state of affairs. There has to be an experience of growing intimacy on every level with your spouse. We should be seeking to capture each other's hearts. It is the same when we come to Christ. If the heart isn't involved, we will hear God complain, "These people ... honor me with their lips, but their hearts are far from me" (Isaiah 29:13). Involving the heart sometimes means coming to terms with our pride. Our haughty hearts bristle at the suggestion that we cannot handle our relationships ourselves, even our relationship with God. Sometimes we act like my young grandchild, who, coming to a heady realization of her own independence, pushes away the helping fingers of her mother who was trying to button all the buttons on her coat: "I can do it myshelf, tankoo."

We stick out our small spiritual chests and boast, "Watch me. I can do it myself! I'll find God, please God, and obey God to the letter—but I'll do it *my* way on *my* terms, and it *won't* be by the way of suffering. I know how to get all my buttons buttoned against the cold wind. I'll figure out how to get to know him more without walking down the road of suffering." So often we are just like the Pharisees: we believe we can get what we want by a meticulous keeping of rules—the rules and regulations of Christianity.

One of the rules of our faith is reading the Bible. Maybe by doing our Bible reading we'll be shielded from trouble. So we keep that rule day by day. However, when following the rules is our focus, we run the risk of spending our daily devotional time with our Bibles but not necessarily with God. Is this possible? Of course. We can read the Bible without allowing it to make an ounce of difference in our hearts or our relationship with God. Our Bible reading must be understood, applied to our lives, mixed with faith, and obeyed before it can affect our hearts and our relationship with God.

In addition to Bible reading, we follow all the other rules as well. We go to church, we worship, and we pray. That's what Christians are supposed to do, right? But do any of these things stop trouble or bring us closer to God on their own? We can go to church and sing any number of songs and hymns and still have no sense of God's presence because our minds are a thousand miles away. No true worship has occurred. Our hearts have not become the sanctuary of God. We may as well have stayed home.

These practices—Bible reading, worship, prayer—aren't talismans; they don't have magical powers that protect us from suffering. Knowing God more doesn't mean merely knowing and following Christian rules—even evangelical rules like Bible reading, prayer, church attendance, and sharing your faith through witnessing. What it comes down to is this: knowing in reality God's life-changing presence and work as he points out our broken image in the mirror of his Word and invites us into a deeper soul knowledge and transformation. It's about having a relationship that reaches down into the depths of our souls and changes us from the inside out so we *want* to keep the rules because it pleases God and not because it pleases the pastor or other leaders in the church. When we practice pleasing God, it results in beginning to keep the rules without even thinking about them.

IT'S WHAT GOD DOES, NOT WHAT WE DO, THAT MAKES THE DIFFERENCE

In a sense, it's true that knowing God will mean that we do more things for him—the more we know him, the more we want to serve him. But Jesus himself said that on the day of judgment, he will say to some who professed to have done incredible works in his name, "I never knew you" (Matthew 7:23). In other words, "You loved the works more than you loved me," Jesus will lament. And this is possible too. As someone once said, "It is frighteningly possible to love the work of the Lord more than the Lord of the work." Like the Pharisees did. Like Paul once did.

The Pharisees and the legalistic Judaizers had hounded Paul wherever he went in the world. They were his fiercest opponents. Yet he had once been one of them. He had believed that you have to keep every piece of the law, plus the bits and pieces his group had added, to know and please God. He discovered that none of it worked to bring about this result at all.

So it is with people today who think that whatever they can do for God will give them access to God. So they must work for God—be good as gold for God, sing in the church choir for God, teach Sunday school kids about God, lead a women's Bible study, go on a mission trip, help the poor, even give themselves in martyrdom for God. Sadly, all of this doesn't give them the heart of God and certainly doesn't provide the key to spiritual intimacy. It doesn't give them the key to heaven's front door or even its back door, for that matter.

It's what *God* can do for me that makes the difference, not what I can do for him. It is not only about working for God but allowing God to work in me so that I serve others because I *want* to, not because I have to. What's more, this work in my heart isn't dependent on me but rather on him. I can't dream it up or pretend it into life; in fact, I can't do anything at all in my own strength—Paul calls this "in the flesh" (Philippians 3:3). It is all to no avail whatsoever.

Moreover, God chooses how he will respond to us and make this "knowing him more" work. I can't twist the Almighty's arm and make him do anything for me at all. I can't make him make me feel good or forgive me. I can't make him answer my prayers. I can't make him give me peace of mind and heart or make the Bible come alive as I read it. It is entirely up to him. The basis of all prayer is "helplessness," says O. Hallesby in his classic book called *Prayer.** I can work myself up into a lather of religious fervor and hang around the church all my waking hours, and it will make no difference. We are dependent on God's grace. We cannot earn our

---

*O. Hallesby, *Prayer* (1931; rev. ed., Minneapolis: Augsburg, 1994), 18.

way into his heart or his heaven, or even into spiritual intimacy, but we can come helplessly and simply ask for his mercy and his help to know him more. It's something like a small child who runs out of strength on a long walk and in the end just gives up, sits down, and looks up hopefully at her father, who bends down and lifts her up.

I have a friend who came to the point of helplessness in a foreign country. She became separated from her group and couldn't speak the language, and she became very frightened. She cried out to God. She was out of ideas, strength, and food. Eventually, her group found her—and all ended well. Later, when they compared notes, her friends discovered that they had begun a new search in the right direction at the exact time my friend had come to the end of her resources and offered her prayers to God.

Paul knew the futility of working hard to make his prayers work. He also knew the futility of doing God's work in his own strength. He found out that he couldn't please God until he came to the end of his own efforts. In essence he concluded, "Everything I did, everything I tried to do, was of no value whatsoever. It was like rubbish. What I needed was Christ—Christ alone" (3:7–8). And Christ is all we need too. We can know him and enjoy him and be empowered "to grasp how wide and long and high and deep is the love of Christ" (Ephesians 3:18). We only have to ask.

THE JOY OF THE LORD IS WHAT MARKS US AS BELIEVERS

The joy of knowing God more, even in the midst of troubles, is a key theme in the book of Philippians. "Rejoice in the Lord," Paul implores again and again. The word "joy" (and variations such as "rejoice") occur fourteen times in this all too short letter.

Remember, Paul wrote this letter from prison. Joy was the outward evidence of the infallible presence of God in Paul's life, and this same joy should be endemic in the body of believers.

In Paul's day, orthodox Jews looked not to joy but circumcision as the outward evidence that demonstrated God's presence in their lives and marked them as Israelites. Circumcision was the mark of the covenant—God's promise that they were his chosen people. Paul said that he was "circumcised on the eighth day," according to the law (Philippians 3:5), but when he found Christ—or rather, when Christ found him on the Damascus road—he realized that outward marks have little to do with interior reality. And so he began to speak of the "circumcision of the heart" as the mark that really matters (Romans 2:29). The markings of our deep relationship with God are shown outwardly in the fruit of our inner life as Christ is formed in us. Joy is one aspect of the fruit of the Spirit that marks us as his children (Galatians 5:22).

NEARLY PERFECT WON'T DO

When it came to following rules and working hard to please God, Paul knew what he was talking about. He was "nearly perfect" when it came to adhering to the Pharisees' values and codes. Talking about his effort to be a perfect Pharisee, he says, "In regard to the law, a Pharisee; … as for legalistic righteousness, faultless" (Philippians 3:5–6).

A few years ago, Stuart and I were invited to speak at a beautiful retirement center in Mexico. Most of the residents were Canadian and American citizens who wanted to retire to the Mexican coast, where they could enjoy the warmer climate. However, as some Christian residents relocated and settled in, they discovered that the center had no chaplain and offered no church services.

Their location on an isolated piece of coastline meant that the nearest church was miles away, and its services were conducted in Spanish. Rather than go without church, they managed to get some of our videotapes and began broadcasting them on a TV in the restaurant/bar/community room on Sunday mornings. To their delight, dozens of people started showing up for "church." At first, all they did each Sunday was listen to the teaching. After a while, they added a simple version of a more complete worship service.

A year or so later, a well-dressed couple introduced themselves to me during coffee hour at our church. After shaking my hand, they asked to meet their pastor. Puzzled, I asked if they were first-time visitors.

"Yes," they said, "and we would like to meet our pastor, Stuart Briscoe."

I found Stuart, and after another round of introductions, we were amazed when the couple invited us to meet *our* congregation in Mexico! So we traveled out for what was an incredible weekend. We met in different apartments every mealtime and in small groups all day. On Sunday we had "real church." People crammed into the community room, but instead of a television, there was a real-live pastor there. Members of the congregation kept coming up and touching Stuart to assure themselves that it was really him!

One afternoon, we had a split session. I taught the women, and Stuart taught the men. I said to the women, "You've been listening to us talk at you all this time. Are there any questions you would like me to try to answer for you about what you have heard? Immediately a sharply dressed elderly woman sitting in the front row said, "Yes, I have a question."

"What is it?" I asked.

"How good do I have to be to get to heaven?" she asked.

"Perfect," I answered without hesitation. There was silence.

Then the woman asked quietly and soberly, "Then who can go?"

That's where we began, and two hours later we closed the session. We had walked through Philippians 3, where Paul explains that heaven is perfect and that we can't go there unless our imperfections have been removed and our sins have been forgiven.

I reminded them that Jesus took our punishment by dying on the cross in our place and that his blood had justified us in God's eyes so we could live with him forever. When asked what the word "justified" meant, I quoted someone's quaint take on the word: "It means '*just as if I'd*' never sinned. It's being perfect."

Doing many good and religious things will never cover over our sin. Paul discovered this truth; I discovered it, and that day in the retirement center, some sweet, wonderful, very religious people discovered it too. Nearly perfect won't do. First, you come to know Jesus as Savior and Lord, next you go deeper in your heart relationship with him, and then the joy comes.

Have you discovered this? Are you trying to live your life as best as you know how, as perfectly as possible? What about all the imperfections of the past? What can we do with those? Only perfect people can go to heaven, or we would spoil it and make it like earth—and God will never allow that.

YOU CAN'T INHERIT GOD

Belonging to the right family, tribe, or nation makes no difference either. Paul said that he was "of the people of Israel, of the tribe of Benjamin, a Hebrew of Hebrews; in regard to the law, a Pharisee" (Philippians 3:5). His point is that it doesn't matter how you were raised. Whether you are a Presbyterian, Anglican, Methodist, Baptist, or free churchman, the denomination you were raised in will not give you a free pass through the pearly gates or produce heart knowledge of God.

Years ago, when we were working with unchurched teens, a young man asked me, "What church do I have to join if I want to have my slate wiped clean? There's a Catholic one near my house and a Methodist place around the corner and a Salvation Army hut opposite my workplace." Then, as an afterthought, he asked, "Where do you go? Which abomination do you belong to?"

I laughed. Of course, he had gotten his words a little mixed up. I explained that denominations are not abominations and that it doesn't really matter which evangelical church you attend—it's a matter of knowing Christ and worshiping him personally in the sanctuary of your heart.

The apostle Paul belonged to the right family who went to the right church. It didn't matter in the end. What matters is to meet Christ in your spirit, as surely as Paul met him in his vision on the road to Damascus, and then to spend the rest of your life getting to know him more and more and more.

So convinced was Paul of this that he set his soul to explore the depths of those things the Holy Spirit explained to him of Christ, and the more he knew, the more he wanted to know—and the more he went after God. He developed the art of spiritual communion with God. After meeting the risen Christ, he lost everything that the world says is important and said it was no big deal compared to the gain of coming to know Christ in an intimate way (see Philippians 3:8).

For Paul, knowing Christ Jesus as his Lord meant experiencing the intimate life with Christ that began at his conversion and continued all the years since then. The challenge and excitement of an ever-growing comprehension of Christ in personal heart knowledge and enjoyment far surpassed any and every experience he had found in a legalistic lifestyle.

THE POWER OF THE RESURRECTION

After Paul talks about the deadness of legalism, he talks about what counteracts deadness — resurrection! Have you ever seen a dead body? If you have, then the power of the resurrection will interest you.

I remember sitting next to my mother as she died. When she had taken her last breath, I just sat there very quietly. I was aware of a spiritual presence in the room, and I knew that God was there. I looked at my mother, or rather the "house" she had lived in. The body of my much-loved mother was motionless. "No life here," I remember saying to myself. "She has gone." And indeed she had, leaving behind the physical part of her I had known and loved for over forty-five years. Looking at her body, I remember wondering, "What power would it take to bring this body of death back to life?" Fast on the heels of that thought came the answer: the power of the resurrection. Yes! Only *that* power could raise a dead body.

Paul talked about knowing such power while he was still alive — the same power that raised Christ from the dead was living in Paul's mortal body. Paul taught that knowing God involves experiencing the power of the resurrection life of Christ. Part of knowing Christ more is experiencing more power to be what we should be and to do what we should do. In Romans, Paul writes, "If the Spirit of him that raised Jesus from the dead is living in you, he who raised Christ from the dead will also give life to your mortal bodies through his Spirit, who lives in you" (Romans 8:11).

This is an amazing verse. It speaks not only of God raising our bodies after death but also of the vital power of his life in us now.

"What did I know about that?" I asked myself on the dark day my mother died. I thought about the power I needed to do the things I was called to do. To go to the places I was called to go to. To speak to the people I was called to speak to. To hold an AIDS baby in my arms, or to speak love into the heart of a refugee. Was there power like that available to me? "Yes!" says Paul.

Paul says he wants to know that power in the nitty-gritty of his own dilemmas. The power to endure, to speak up for Christ with courage and boldness. To persevere and press on and on and on. Knowing Christ more means knowing more and more of his resurrection power as we appropriate the saving life of Christ. It means experiencing the power that proceeds from the living Savior.

This means counting myself dead to my own self-effort and alive to the power of God. Where does all this happen? On your knees, hanging on to God for all you're worth, reaching for the hand of God to steady you when you're about to fall down, counting on what I call "God-spiritability" to carry on carrying on. I want to know more of that. Don't you?

So how do I begin to know it?

- I spend some time thinking about all of this.
- I tell God where I see myself.
- I confess my own futile efforts at being spiritual without reference to the Spirit.
- I ask him to show me where to begin.
- I begin.

Undoubtedly, as I've already said, the Bible and prayer feature in the answer. We need to make a plan—our own spiritual plan. What are you going to do to know Christ more where Bible study, prayer, meditation, and worship are concerned? Which part of prayer will you decide on? Intercession? Worship and praise? Confession and repentance? Faith and fasting?

Which part of the Bible will you study for the purpose of finding Christ there? How will you study it? Take a course? Read a book? Buy a commentary? Memorize an epistle—Philippians perhaps?

Ask yourself, "Where am I suffering at the moment? How can I use this suffering to know Christ better?" Talk to the Lord about it. Think it through in silence, inviting the Spirit to calm the noise and confusion inside you.

Ponder this: What sort of Jesus-lover and glory-giver do I want to be after this is over? What do I want to share with others from this experience? Do I want to tell how God has given me strength I didn't know was even possible to have? Will I be able to teach people not to waste the pain instead of demanding that God "kiss it and make it better" at once? Am I able to allow the suffering of this present time to be the meeting place for God and me, a place where I might get to know him as I've never known him?

Paul testified to a depth of spiritual intimacy that he knew through the fellowship of sharing in Christ's sufferings, the power of the resurrection life while facing death, and the ability to consider himself dead to himself and alive to all that Christ was for him as he came to know Christ more. It's an art—a spiritual art—to do the work and submit to the discipline, but it's worth every single bit of effort.

QUESTIONS FOR REFLECTION
AND DISCUSSION

1. Read Philippians 3:12–14. Paul points out that Christianity is not an outward exercise but rather the spiritual intimacy of the soul—an interior "knowing" made possible only by God's saving grace. What do you think Paul means in verse 10 by "knowing Christ"

   - in the power of Christ's resurrection?

   - in the fellowship of sharing in Christ's sufferings?

   - in Christ's death?

2. Discuss (or journal) your response to some of these statements and ideas found in this chapter. Which ones especially spoke to you?

   - I want to know Christ more.

   - Spiritual closeness often happens in the university of life's bitter, not better, moments.

   - As we follow Christ, there will inevitably be wounds and scars. What will we do when we are wounded and hurt? Can we allow the work of the Spirit to take us deeper in our knowledge of God because of the winds of adversity?

   - To know more about the rules doesn't necessarily lead to knowing more of God deep inside or being rewarded with exemption from suffering. It doesn't shield you from trouble.

   - Nearly perfect won't do.

- The challenge and excitement of an ever-growing comprehension of Christ in personal heart knowledge and enjoyment far surpassed any and every experience [Paul] had found in a legalistic lifestyle.

3. List the steps you can take to begin to know Christ more. For example:

- Respond to suffering instead of reacting against it.

- Let the Bible read you instead of you reading the Bible.

- Appropriate the power of God for a situation where you are weak.

THOUGHTS FOR PRAYER

1. Spend some time in silent prayer.

2. Pray with your group (if you're studying this book in a group) or by yourself about spiritual intimacy in your life, in your family, in your church, and in the church in the United States.

CHAPTER 5

the spiritual art of
tenacity

One thing I do: Forgetting what is behind and straining toward
what is ahead, I press on toward the goal to win the prize
for which God has called me heavenward in Christ Jesus.
Philippians 3:13–14

The spiritual art of tenacity is a learned art. You cannot learn it unless you have something to be tenacious about, something to care deeply about—being a Christian, for example. We learn to be persistent, or tenacious, when we have to press on through life's difficulties. Daily challenges and struggles in the Christian life and the experience of being mistreated because of a profession of faith in Christ are examples of opportunities to develop tenacity. The word "tenacious" can be defined as "holding fast," "being tough," "being persistent or stubborn," "clinging or adhering to something." In a word, *stickability*. Sticking with someone or something to the end—like sticking with Christ and his call to us to follow him.

THE ART OF FINISHING

Paul is a perfect example of stickability. He uses the image of a footrace to make his point. As far as Paul was concerned, his race wasn't complete until he reached the finish line—that is, until death came calling. He was not about to quit, no matter what happened to him. Paul was able to say at the end of his life, "I have fought the good fight, I have finished the race, I have kept the faith. Now there is in store for me the crown of righteousness, which the Lord, the righteous Judge, will award to me on that day" (2 Timothy 4:7–8).

Pressing on and finishing things are virtues lacking in our culture. My husband says that Western culture militates against discipleship. I think I know what he means. Hardly anybody finishes anything anymore. The kids are signed up for a YMCA class. If they don't want to get out of bed one Saturday morning, they don't go to class. Perhaps we ourselves are in an exercise regime or have started yet another diet. How long does it last? Even if we've paid the fee for the club or bought the prepackaged food for the diet, how well do we finish what we start?

It can be the same with our spiritual disciplines—reading the Bible, attending a study, beginning one more season of prayer. We drop out when the class is halfway through or when the book we're reading begins to bore us. We don't finish. Finishing is an art. It takes discipline to persist. The famous nineteenth-century preacher Charles Spurgeon said, "By perseverance the snail reached the ark."

Stuart and I frequently teach at pastors' conferences. We have discovered that, no matter what you do, people leave before the official end. You can make the conference shorter, but it makes no difference. On the last day, attendance inevitably shrinks. Even if the conference is just a one-day event, people will leave before the last session. What's behind this behavior?

The same thing often happens when we come to faith matters. Even if we run well for a few years, we then slow to a near stop or run off the track altogether and retire from the race. This is the case especially as we grow older. We just get tired—tired of serving, tired of attending two worship services a week, tired of arriving on time or staying until the benediction.

There seems to be an increasing spiritual fatigue among us. There is a difference between being tired *in* the work of the Lord and tired *of* the work of the Lord. When we get tired *of* the work of the Lord, we are in danger of quitting the race altogether. We will probably be tired *in* it as long as there aren't enough hands to share the load. But as Paul said, "Though outwardly we are wasting away, yet inwardly we are being renewed day by day" (2 Corinthians 4:16).

Listen to Paul: "If I am to go on living in the body, this will mean fruitful labor for me" (Philippians 1:22). Although he was bone weary, he was as young in spirit and passion as when he first met the living Christ. He was an old man with a young heart. Dynamic and fruitful labor went hand in hand for Paul. He was tenacious, and he persisted—he preached and taught, exhorted and encouraged, rebuked and challenged. He traveled and visited and never gave up building the church until his last breath. In a nutshell, he finished!

THERE IS NO SPIRITUAL RETIREMENT FOR THE CHRISTIAN

The danger is that the older we get, the more ready we are to quit. We may well retire from our jobs, but there is no spiritual retirement for the disciple of Jesus. How could there be? Here is Paul, the aged one, pressing on. He is certainly old and worn, tired and sick, but he is strong in his determination to die with his boots on. Persistent and stubborn, he's sitting in a horrible place, having had his freedom taken away for no other reason than that he is a follower of Christ. But just listen to him: "I keep working toward that day when I finally will be all that Christ Jesus saved me for and wants me to be" (Philippians 3:14, my translation). "I'm pressing on," declares Paul. In other words, "I am practicing the spiritual art of tenacity." He wants his present suffering to make him a more effective minister and a better racer with a stronger track record. He thinks about other old saints around, and he hopes that they will take heart when they hear about his commitment to finish well.

Caleb is an Old Testament example of the same kind of spiritual tenacity we see in Paul. Caleb fought alongside Joshua until they had taken possession of the Promised Land. When he entered the land, he was eighty years old. As parcels of land were being distributed to the tribes of Israel, Caleb came to Joshua to ask for land for his tribe. Which land? The rolling hills for his cattle? The fertile rich lowlands? No. "Give me this mountain," he says (Joshua 14:12 KJV). Any farmer worth his salt knows that mountains represent a whole lot of blood, sweat, and tears. Caleb is eighty, and instead of asking for the ease of conquering the foothills, he demands a mountain. That's exciting!

I am humbled by this. I want to be like Caleb. I want to press on, for the best is yet to be. When I'm eighty, I want to be found saying, "Give me this mountain." What fueled the flame in Joshua's and Caleb's hearts? Their secret is written in Scripture: they "followed the LORD ... wholeheartedly" (Joshua 14:8). No retirement in Canaan's rocking chairs for these two veterans!

Tenacity is following the Lord with your whole heart. Not with halfhearted steps but all the way home. The Lord commands us to follow his steps. How do we do this?

IN HIS STEPS

It was wintertime when we moved from England to the United States in 1970. We were used to a temperate climate and had never experienced such *intemperate* weather. A Wisconsin storm covered the ground with two feet of snow on the day we arrived. We were not equipped for any of this, but that didn't keep us from getting out in the glorious, white fluffy stuff and having a great time. Stuart took our three children to the top of a big hill behind our house. He ran down the hill with huge strides all the way to the bottom. Then he shouted up to the kids, "Now you try. Put your feet in my footsteps." Well, they tried their very best, but there was no way they could follow in his steps.

Stuart climbed to the top of the hill again. One by one, he had David, Judy, and Pete put their feet on his feet while he put his strong hands beneath their arms. Then he bounded down the hill again with giant strides. The kids squealed in delight. There they were, resting in their father's arms and walking in his footsteps. What a picture!

Consider these words of the apostle Paul: "I can do everything through [Christ] who gives me strength" (Philippians 4:13). God asks us to walk in his steps, to make the journey of life all the way down the hill. There is no way we can do this in our own strength. We are too small. We are too weak. But in Christ we can. Yes, we can! We can come all the way down the hill. We need to practice the art of running down the hill, of trying to put our feet in his footsteps, of following in his way. We need to be obedient to the Father's voice and do as we are instructed. We need to rest in his arms and let him carry us. Amazingly enough, this takes spiritual tenacity. What takes tenacity? *Resting.* Really? Yes, it requires surrender to rest in God's strength. Believe it or not, it also takes practice. It requires a decision to trust God and to follow in his steps—even when it seems as though what you really want is to run down the hill all by yourself.

So what about Paul's heart? What kept him going? He knew that, no matter how old and weak he was, he could rest in God's arms and follow in God's steps. How does he relentlessly center his attention on the course ahead of him without passing out on the running track? He says he is holding firmly to Christ, who is holding firmly to him: "I press on to take hold of that for which Christ Jesus took hold of me" (3:12). He is clinging to his Savior, his heart is aflame for God, and he is all about finishing the race and keeping the faith. He has a goal, and he is reaching for the prize. This sort of tenacity is a spiritual art, and it begins with your faith.

ATTITUDE ADJUSTMENTS

Attitudes are the key to any spiritual art. Our attitude toward God is vital. Do we trust him? Do we believe—really believe—that he is strong enough to carry us down the hill? Do we think that maybe he needs some help from us? Some of us need a tune-up—an attitude adjustment. An attitude is a mind-set, a disposition. The Holy Spirit can help us with this. We can pray for a positive attitude toward the Lord instead of a negative one, and we can follow Paul's example by looking at our circumstances positively rather than negatively (see chapter 1).

What circumstance do you need God to carry you through? Is it a difficult situation at work or church? Do you need to sort out a family dilemma? Perhaps you've given up on a situation because you have been trying and trying, and somehow your efforts only seem to make matters worse. Maybe you prayed about it, but God didn't appear as a genie to fix it, so you took things back into your own hands. It could be that your attitude toward God is that he is a helper rather than a carrier. It takes an attitude adjustment to say, "Without him I can do nothing. So I will trust him completely to carry the responsibility of this."

When I was a young mother, I felt the confines of being a stay-at-home mom. I chafed under the circumstances until I changed my attitude. I prayed that the Lord would help me see the positives in the situation, and I began to praise him for them. Praising him for the positives helped me to look for more advantages. One advantage was learning to allow God to carry responsibilities for me. I tried to ask him about all major decisions involving the children. It wasn't that I stopped thinking and trying to figure out the right things to do, but I often felt overwhelmed—I wanted to be a perfect mother who did everything right. At last I gave the responsibility to God and let him have the worry of it. I learned to trust him to carry me down the hill in his steps day by day. And the Spirit encouraged me. Once my attitude changed, I began to take advantage of my stay-at-home years for God, for my family, and for myself. This helped me finish the parenting part of my race. I didn't do it perfectly, of course, but I did it. I finished my laps and didn't opt out.

"It's never over until it's over," is Paul's message to us. "I haven't got it all together. I haven't arrived. There is still a lot of race to run. There are challenges both outside of me and inside of me." Paul is not too big to admit that he is still on a steep learning curve. He is learning to know Christ in ways he has never known him before, to endure hardship as a good soldier of Jesus Christ, to be patient, understanding, and compassionate with his persecutors. He is appropriating the saving life of Christ for every eventuality and in every stage of the race. In short, Paul is learning the art of tenacity. He is ever the student of Christ. Paul trusts Christ, and he rests in Christ's power and strength.

There are things to learn about Jesus as long as we live and move and have our being (see Acts 17:28). We never graduate with a "perfect Christian" certificate this side of heaven. Like Caleb, we need to behave as though age isn't particularly relevant. Like Paul, we need to endure hardship as discipline (Hebrews 12:7), be thankful, and run on.

When we keep ourselves and our situations in perspective (with positive attitudes and trust in God) and are humble enough to acknowledge that we are not the bionic Christian persons others believe us to be, then we are in the right mode to grow. Paul understood his proud rebel heart. Circumstances that humble us help us to learn and grow. Can we say with sincerity, "I haven't arrived spiritually, so I'll press on"? Like Paul, are we focusing all of our energies on this "one thing" (Philippians 3:13)?

None of us have arrived. To believe we have made it as a parent, child, Bible teacher, ministry leader, Sunday school teacher, butcher, baker, or candlestick maker sets us up for a fall. If we allow God to show us ourselves as he sees us, we understand the devious nature of our sorry hearts.

The struggle to walk in the Spirit and not in the flesh will never come to an end until we are safely home. There is still a ton to learn. There are children to raise for Christ and his kingdom, people to weep for, countries to reach where Christ has not been preached. There are churches to build, leaders to train, prayers to be prayed, and people to stand in the gap until the next generation of teachers and evangelists comes along. We must help the helpless and care for the lost. Knowing that we haven't arrived in our calling, ministry goals, and spiritual life is an impetus to press on until we do. This was the driving motivation that consumed Paul, and this was why he said, "One thing I do."

HANDLING REBELLION IN THE RANKS

One way in which God helps us to think about ourselves as we ought so that we will persevere is by allowing us to have opponents—often within the church itself. Paul's opponents in the church were delighted when he was put in jail. They saw their opportunity and took advantage of Paul's confinement for their own aggrandizement. They wanted to preach. They thought that they could do it better than he could. A spirit of competition predominated. Some of these preachers were jealous of Paul. They didn't like the way he taught. "Now," they thought, "we can take over and do it right." Paul's confinement provided a golden opportunity.

Paul was told about what was happening. Instead of over-reacting or being hurt, he simply said, "What does it matter? The important thing is that in every way ... Christ is preached" (Philippians 1:18). Paul was so free from wanting things his own way or doing things with a wrong motive that he didn't give a thought to his own feelings. "Christ is preached"—that was all he cared about. It wasn't who did the preaching or how the preaching was done that mattered, but rather that it was done at all—that the gospel was proclaimed. That is a big man talking.

In the 1960s, Stuart and I left our marketplace careers to work with a Christian youth mission in the United Kingdom. Stuart was treasurer of the mission organization. He had been a lay preacher for years, but the mission was only vaguely aware of this. He had been on the inspection staff of a large bank before going into full-time ministry work, and so he was invited to take over the finances of the mission organization.

In the evenings, hundreds of teens gathered to listen to a Christian speaker. Stuart oversaw the meeting, sometimes led worship from the piano, greeted the kids at the door, handed out chorus sheets, and then sat back and listened to whomever was preaching.

"Surely Stuart will be asked to speak to the kids," I thought. "He's terrific with them." Stuart knew, and I knew, that this was why we had laid down our careers to be part of this ministry. But he was never asked to speak.

It began to get to me. When I voiced my frustrations, Stuart said, "Jill, it won't matter in a hundred years who handed out the hymnbooks and who stood on the platform." In other words, my husband was saying, "What does it matter? Christ is being preached, and in this I rejoice." That was a big man speaking, and it was a salutary lesson for me. Months later, the visiting speaker was ill, and the leader of our mission said to Stuart, "Someone told me you've been doing some speaking. Why don't you take the speaker's place?" After that first meeting, our leader included him on the preaching team. The rest, as they say, is history.

It would have been easy for Stuart to criticize the speakers and say in his heart, "I could do it better." Or he could see this as an opportunity to show humility and focus on the most important thing—not who was doing the teaching but the fact that the teaching was being done.

As I quit seething, I began to pray for the speakers. I stopped criticizing and started being thankful that there were so many who wanted to preach the gospel. This attitude helped me to carry on in whatever capacity God had placed us in.

If we had been in Rome with Paul during visiting hours at the prison, we might have had a conversation on this issue:

"How is it going, Paul?"

"One thing I do."

"And just what is this one thing, Paul?"

"Well," he would answer, "the first thing is forgetting, the next thing is pressing on, and the third thing is tenaciously exercising my faith to finish well and to get the prize."

"That's three things, Paul."

"Three in one," he would have replied. "The main thing is the goal. These three things will be the way I will meet my objective and collect the prize.

"And what is the prize, Paul?"

"Jesus, my Savior! See, he is waiting at the finish line for me. He will greet me and say, 'Well done, good and faithful servant.' Can you imagine what a prize that will be?"

WE'RE NOT HOME YET

Paul knew that the prize was at the finish line. So often we want the prize now—as we run along the way.

I heard a true story about an elderly missionary couple who had spent their entire adult lives on the mission field. They had paid a heavy price with regard to their health and their family, but they stayed the course. The time came for retirement. It was in the days when missionaries went away and returned by boat.

When they had left England at the beginning of their missionary career, the platform at Euston Station had been packed with friends and church people, who gave them a grand send-off. A band played hymns and the group of believers prayed and sent them on their way with flags flying. It was a fabulous memory. Now they were sailing home after a lifetime of faithful work.

There was a celebrity on board, and when the boat came into the harbor, they could see that the dockside was crowded with people. Banners were flying, and the band was playing. They watched as the gangplank was lowered, searching the crowd for the mission welcoming committee. The celebrity was welcomed with due pomp and circumstance, and then it was over, and the rest of the passengers began to disembark. Still the two old servants of the Lord searched the dock. They didn't see one familiar face.

Unfortunately, the dates had gotten mixed up, and the reception had been mistakenly set for the following day. Of course, the two old-timers had no way of knowing this. So there they were, standing alone on the dockside with their trunks and all their worldly goods. They sat on their trunks and cried. They had come home to this? As they sat there holding on to each other, bewildered and hurt beyond measure, the husband said, "Let's be quiet and try to hear what God is saying. So they held each other tight and stood in the Lord's presence on the quayside, oblivious of the activity around them. The old man opened his eyes, and they were shining. "Darling," he said, "God spoke to me. He told me, 'You're not home yet.' "

They began to laugh—a great, glad joy-laugh. It wasn't over yet. There was still time to serve the Lord. There were people to encourage and candidates to train and send out in their place. One day the band would be out, and the Lord would be on the quayside of heaven to welcome them home—but not yet, and not now. They picked up their things and set off for the train station, light of heart, to finish their journey to the village where they would live.

SHOOTING ADRENALINE INTO OUR SOULS

Paul warns us there will be many discouraging moments before we're through. But he tells us not to lose heart. The race is never over until it's over, and running it will require us to learn the spiritual art of tenacity. Where will we find the strength? What happens when we find ourselves running out of steam? Paul would tell us, "Run on in the strength the Lord gives you. And *that* strength never runs out. You can do all things through Christ, who gives you strength." Remember the snowy hill in our backyard? Rest in the Lord's arms and follow in his steps, and he will carry you home.

So how does it work when we are just ordinary folks? Where will we "little people" find such strength to finish? We aren't the apostle Paul. We aren't the mighty Caleb or those veteran missionaries. But Jesus is the same Jesus! The strength and encouragement come from observing Jesus and remembering how he ran his race and finished his course. They come as we follow in his steps.

Jesus left no unfinished business when he went home to his Father. He was able to say, "I finished. I finished what I started. I finished the work my heavenly Father gave me to do." On the cross, he shouted, "It is finished" (John 19:30). He was not shouting, "*I* am finished," but "*It* is finished"—the redemption of the human race has been accomplished.

We must keep our eyes on Jesus, who both began and finished the race. "*That*," says Eugene Peterson, "will shoot adrenaline into your souls!" (Hebrews 12:3 MSG). When you find yourself flagging, go over that wonderful story once again, bit by bit. Take an afternoon to read through the Gospels at a sitting. Think about "that long litany of hostility [Jesus] plowed through" for you (Hebrews 12:3 MSG), the race of redemption he ran for humankind. He finished his course; now we must finish ours.

STRIP DOWN, START RUNNING,
AND NEVER STOP

We are urged by the author of Hebrews to keep our eyes on Jesus, and we are also reminded that, while we run the race of life on earth, those in the heavenlies are keeping their eyes on us. Pioneers cheer us on, watching us from "Ever-land." They blazed the way for us. They are the people who have gone before us, who loved the Lord and have finished well. They have become spectators in the stands of heaven: "Therefore, since we are surrounded by such a great cloud of witnesses, let us throw off everything that hinders and the sin that so easily entangles, and let us run with persever-ance the race marked out for us" (Hebrews 12:1). What does this mean?

Eugene Peterson presents it to us in modern language:

It means we'd better get on with it. Strip down, start running—and never quit! No extra spiritual fat, no parasitic sins. Keep your eyes on *Jesus*, who both began and finished this race we're in. Study how he did it. Because he never lost sight of where he was headed—that exhilarating finish in and with God—he could put up with anything along the way: cross, shame, what-ever. And now he's *there*, in the place of honor, right alongside God.

Hebrews 12:1–3 MSG

I love the phrase "strip down, start running—and never quit." If you're going to run a race, you need to strip down, to put off all the things that will hinder your running—such things as "sin clothes" and other things that slow us down. You don't run a race in a snowmobile suit! Many things hinder us from staying in the race—some are good things, and some are bad. But that's where spiritual tenacity comes in. We just keep pressing on. We never quit. We lay aside the things that cause our feet to become tangled and that keep us from running without encumbrances.

Some of the hindrances can be things from our past. That's why Paul says we have to work at "forgetting what is behind" (Philippians 3:13). How do you handle hindrances from your past? Are you still dragging them around like a ball and chain? They need to be dealt with so you can move forward unencumbered. It may be wise to talk with someone about this—perhaps a wise Christian who knows you well or a pastor or counselor who can help you to be set free from past failure, shame, and guilt. You need to stop looking over your shoulder so you can look forward to the next leg of the race God has marked out for you.

STOP LOOKING OVER YOUR SHOULDER

I find looking over my shoulder a real hindrance. I do it all the time. My husband says that we—he and I—have more history than future. It's easy for us to live in the past. I'm a rather negative thinker, and so I tend to dwell on the bad things from the past—the failures and the pain, the times I didn't run well, the times I got lazy and slowed my pace to a near stop—rather than on the good things. It's hard to forget the sharp word that caused hurt, a parting of the ways with a colleague, and the missed opportunities that will never come my way again. Paul says you can't run a race twice, and you can't run it continually looking over your shoulder. You will surely trip and fall. We have to move on and leave the mistakes and sins of the past at the foot of the cross of Christ.

I can imagine that Paul was tempted to spend most of his time in prison regretting the time he persecuted the church. The faces of the children whose parents he killed must have haunted him.

But he kept his eyes on what was ahead and trusted his past to God. Leaving his terrible sins at Calvary, he pressed on. The end of the race was in sight for Paul. He could see the finish line and hear the roar of the cloud of witnesses in the stands. "I leave the past behind," he says. Have we?

Have we left behind the marriage that fell apart? The argument we had with someone who was killed in an accident before we could make amends? Have we moved on from the spell of unfaithfulness that no one knows about? Can we confess it and move on? Did we pay back the debt we owe? If not, why not do it now, so we can stop looking over our shoulder? Are we obsessed by a child who is missing from our lives through his or her own bad choices, or a parent who is not a believer and won't listen to us? What is behind us that keeps us from looking ahead? Turn around, and then go forward. Don't miss the moment.

TENACIOUSLY LOOK UPWARD AND ONWARD

Unlike Paul, most of us don't know when our race will be over. Somehow we expect to live to a ripe old age. In fact, we never expect to die. There is an incredible 104-year-old woman who lives in a rest home near our church. She came to Christ at the age of ninety-eight. Our pastor to seniors told me that this woman doesn't want to die—she wants to live! You're never ready, or so it seems. When someone close to us dies, we get a wake-up call, especially if the person is young. We may have a few sobering moments contemplating the brevity of life, but soon the funeral is over and life resumes. The writer of Ecclesiastes says, "You learn more at a funeral than at a feast" (Ecclesiastes 7:2 MSG). That's because death wonderfully focuses our attention on what life is all about.

However, because we don't know when our day is done, we somehow cultivate this belief that death can happen to everyone else but us. It could be tomorrow, of course, but we simply refuse to believe it. No one knows the length of the course ahead of us—no one, that is, but God himself. He knows. And he tells us that we won't live forever down here. As the old gospel song puts it, "This world is not my home; I'm just a-passin' through." With this in mind, God wants us to forget what's behind and look on to what is ahead. We need to tenaciously look upward and onward, refusing to take one single day for granted. The time is short; the days are evil (see Ephesians 5:16). There's work to be done and not enough people to do it.

At the beginning of his Christian life, Paul's message was essentially this: "I'm off and running, and I'm not turning back." How did he do it? By relentlessly centering his energies and interests on the course ahead of him. He looked upward to Jesus, the author and perfecter of his faith (Hebrews 12:2), and onward to the goal (Philippians 3:14). He stayed focused, and that's what we must do. At the end of his life, Paul hadn't changed his focus or his pace.

WATCHING OUT FOR THE TEAM

As we run our race, we also need to keep track of those who are out there, running the same course.

This race of life is not a relay race, where you pass the baton and you're done. It's more like an Olympic marathon, only you're not running alone—you have a team from your country running with you. You need to be aware of your teammates, know how they're doing, and check up on them. Paul's teammates were

Timothy, Epaphroditus, and Luke. Paul kept track of them. He looked out for them, even though they had come to Rome to look out for him.

I love the makeup of Paul's team. Epaphroditus had been sent from the church at Philippi with a gift of money for Paul. He was a leader there. It had cost the church to have to carry on without him for this time, but they were willing to send their best. It cost both the church and this man to come to Paul. Risking his life, he had gotten sick and nearly died (Philippians 2:27, 30). As you can imagine, this was an added sorrow for Paul. Epaphroditus survived, however, and Paul writes to tell the church back home about this answer to prayer: "he ... almost died. But God had mercy on him" (2:27).

Imagine the cost to Paul. In his dire situation, three leaders and team members must have been priceless companions. But Paul looked out for his team first and not only sent Epaphroditus back to his home church; he told the church that he would soon send Timothy as well (2:23).

In a side comment, Paul tells the believers in Philippi that he knows of no one who cares for their well-being like Timothy (2:20). Timothy had a huge concern for the church in Philippi. Then, of course, there was his dear Dr. Luke, who stuck with Paul through thick and thin and who wrote for us the history of Jesus (Luke's gospel) and of Paul (the book of Acts).

Here we have a beautiful picture of a team of warriors—high-ranking soldiers of the faith who loved the church, loved Paul, and loved each other. They put each other before their own well-being and ran their race with tenacity, regardless of the personal price they would pay. They ran the race together, watching out for each other as they went. Do we do that? Or are we so absorbed with our own lives and ministries that we selfishly care for our own things, using team members for our own purposes and demanding that we come first?

How is your team doing? Your committee? Your volunteers? Your family? The people around you who partner with you in whatever capacity in which you serve the Lord and his community? Do we use people, albeit unintentionally, because we have such pressing needs ourselves? We need to follow Paul's example as we build a team of self-giving leaders and show the way by our own attitude. Paul knew his men. He knew exactly how each of them was doing in the race. He was far more concerned with *how* they were doing than with *what* they were doing.

When my husband served as senior pastor at a large church, he would sit down with each staff member once a year for an update. His first question was, "How are you doing?" not, "What are you doing?" His office door was always open—unless he was counseling. He walked around a lot, being available and accessible. He cared for his team. Who was on Paul's team when he was in prison at Rome? We don't know who else had access to him there, but we do know that these three men did. These men were veteran runners. But you don't become a veteran overnight. This is where the all-important aspect of training comes in.

TROUBLE IS TRAINING

The writer to the Hebrews follows Paul's analogy of the footrace of life by telling his readers that trouble isn't punishment—it's training. After exhorting his listeners "to run with perseverance the race marked out for us" and "fix our eyes on Jesus, the author and perfecter of our faith" (Hebrews 12:1, 2), the writer urges, "Endure hardship as discipline; God is treating you as sons.... No discipline seems pleasant at the time, but painful. Later on, however, it produces a harvest of righteousness and peace for those who have been trained by it" (12:7, 11). It helps me to know that I am in a race I must finish and that the trouble that comes is simply ongoing training. The hard things that happen to me are *not* God's punishment for not doing things properly but rather God's discipline to train me for the race.

So how are you doing? Did something hinder you from running well? What happened? Did you turn your ankle? Undergo a bad fall? Can you pick yourself up from the sidelines and get back on track? Go on; get up. Start back in again. It's allowed!

Paul says to us, "Start again. Forget what tripped you up. Forget what's behind you. Stay focused on what's ahead, and press on. Go for it. Finish the course, keep the faith, and finish well." The Spirit of Jesus who went before you lives in you. He has all you need and all it will take. Draw on his strength. Stay in training all of your life. Get up early. Meet with your coach, the pioneer of your faith. Ask him how he did it. Exercise your mind, your soul, your heart. Get fit; stay fit. Eat right. Discipline your life.

Jesus told us that this race would be an obstacle course. He ran his race and had to endure the jeering instead of cheering, the booing and hissing and spitting in his face, but he endured to the end. How did Jesus do it? By spending much time with the Father. He reveled in his presence, even if he had to get up at dawn to escape the crowds in order to do it. He was strengthened by angels and empowered by the Spirit, and he pressed on for our sakes. We are told to "consider him" (Hebrews 12:3). That will do wonders for our spirits. "Watch me," Jesus tells us. "Follow me home, little child. Lean on me when you're spent; draw strength from me when you are weak. I will nourish you when you faint because of fatigue. Take joy in me, 'for the joy of the LORD is your strength'" (Nehemiah 8:10).

RUNNING THE RACE WITH PATIENCE

"God will give us the strength we need to run the race with great endurance and patience," Paul tells us (Colossians 1:11, my translation). Patience is spiritual tenacity that won't lie down and die. It springs from our love relationship with Christ, from the spiritual intimacy learned day by day and moment by moment.

Many times in my fifty-plus years of ministry I have wanted to quit the race. I have been exhausted not only physically and mentally but also spiritually and emotionally. Sometimes I have been frightened by a hostile crowd or overwhelmed by responsibilities. Other times, I have been worried about team members around me who weren't running well and were just spiritually bone tired of it all. And at still other times, I've been heartbroken about those who have quit altogether. But in those times I know that, no matter what other people do, I can't stop, slow down, or look anywhere but upward and onward. There is a prize waiting for me. It is my "well done, good and faithful servant." That's what I want above all else on earth. So I press on toward the goal. Will you?

QUESTIONS FOR REFLECTION
AND DISCUSSION

1. Paul describes his Christian life as a footrace. How do you forget what is behind and center your energies and interests on the course ahead of you? Do you keep looking over your shoulder? Read and ponder Philippians 3:13–14.

2. Do you experience your spiritual life more as a relay race, a sprint, or a marathon? Up to this point, has it been an individual event or a team event?

3. According to Paul, what is the goal and what is the prize in this race of life? Read and ponder Philippians 3:14.

4. Eugene Peterson's translation of Philippians 3:16–17 (MSG) reads, "So let's keep focused on the goal, those of us who want everything God has for us.... Keep track of those you see running this same course, headed for this same goal." How do we help those on the team who are lagging?

5. Hebrews 12:1 (MSG) reads, "Strip down, start running—and never quit!" Which part of this is the hardest for you? What might it mean for you to "strip down"? What hinders you from carrying out this teaching from Scripture?

6. Look up the following verses: 1 Timothy 4:16; Hebrews 10:36; James 1:12. Which fits your situation today?

THOUGHTS FOR PRAYER

1. Pray for the children and young people you know who are hindered in their race at the present time.

2. Pray for Christians who, like Paul was, are being persecuted. Pray they will be tenacious and finish well.

3. Pray for those who are modern-day equivalents of Epaphroditus, Timothy, and Luke—those who risk their lives to support the persecuted church.

CHAPTER 6

the spiritual art of
maturity

All of us who are mature
should take such a view of things.
Philippians 3:15

"Maturity" refers to "the state or condition of being fully grown or developed." Paul often expressed his prayer that Christ would be fully formed in believers' lives (see Romans 8:29; Galatians 4:19; Ephesians 4:13, 15; Colossians 1:27). Spiritual maturity is the part of the Spirit's art that makes us Christlike. It doesn't happen without us *working out* what the Spirit is *working in* (see Philippians 2:12–13). God's purpose in coming into our hearts in the first place is to grow us up as believers in Jesus. The Spirit desires that we should grow to maturity. We are to live maturely, think maturely, minister maturely, and lead maturely.

A baby is not intended to remain a baby but to grow into an adult. Paul exhorts, "Continue to work out your salvation with fear and trembling, for it is God who works in you to will and to act according to his good purpose" (Philippians 2:12–13). Part of his good purpose is that we should grow up to be like his Son, the Lord Jesus Christ.

ARE YOU HAPPY
WITH YOUR SPIRITUAL SIZE?

We were visiting friends—a family that had been close to us at one point but that we hadn't seen since they moved away. Now the kids were all talking at once, and we were catching up.

Duncan, the youngest and littlest child, couldn't get a word in edgewise. His dad, noticing Duncan's valiant effort to have his turn, said, "Tell Uncle Stuart what you want to be when you grow up." Overwhelmed by the sudden attention and aware of the other children's impatience, Duncan thought quickly. And then, very succinctly, he summed it up. What did he want to be when he grew up? "Bigger!" he announced firmly.

We all looked at the child thoughtfully. We could see where that came from. If he were bigger, he could join in and not be number four on the totem pole. He could get a word in edgewise. He could be part of the big people's conversation in the big people's world and be a big person in his own right. Being as big as his sisters and brothers, and even as big as his dad and mom one day, was a natural goal.

What do you want to be when you grow up spiritually? Bigger? Do you want to be mature in Christ? Or are you happy with your current spiritual size? Are you growing up to be like Christ? Christlikeness in all dimensions of who we are and what we do is our aim.

Practically speaking, our Christlikeness should affect every part of our lives. We should be like Christ in our families, our marriages, our singleness, our jobs, our play, our service. This metamorphosis doesn't happen in the twinkling of an eye. It takes a lifetime. And it takes work. We are to "work out" what God is "working in." Did you see that? It is a *workout*!

If babies don't grow up to become adults, we regard it as an aberration. If Christians who are born again don't grow up, this is an aberration as well. Paul uses the human growth process as an analogy in his epistles. He talks about being a child and speaking, thinking, and reasoning as a child, but then growing up to become a man, at which time he puts childish ways behind him (1 Corinthians 13:11). To think or speak as a child is charming and expected of a child, but if we are thinking and acting like children when we are grown, it becomes obnoxious.

This was the problem in the Corinthian church. The growth in church membership was extraordinary in the city of Corinth, but the Christians in the churches were behaving childishly. God had given this church many miraculous gifts—the gift of tongues and interpretation of tongues, healing, and dramatic charismatic manifestations of the Spirit. The people treated the gifts of the Spirit as toys, not tools to use to grow the church, and Paul had to write them and tell them to grow up.

Members of the Philippian church were behaving childishly too—the two women who couldn't get along and who bickered like children (Philippians 4:2), and the men who competed for preaching opportunities while Paul was in jail (1:15–17). One of the things we expect from mature people, especially Christians, is to stop bickering and get along with each other. Paul had to deal with this kind of immaturity in many of the churches he planted.

GROWING LIKE JESUS

When Jesus went up to the Feast of the Passover in Jerusalem at the age of twelve, he stayed behind to talk with the teachers in the temple as his family left for home (Luke 2:42–43). His parents didn't realize that he wasn't with them. When they discovered his absence, they returned to Jerusalem to search for him. After his parents found Jesus talking to the scholars in the temple—and he reminded them that he needed to be about his Father's business—he went home with Mary and Joseph and "was obedient to them" (2:51). The Bible tells us, "And Jesus grew in wisdom and stature, and in favor with God and men" (2:52).

As Jesus grew up, he grew in four dimensions—in wisdom (intellectually), in stature (physically), in favor with God (spiritually), and in favor with people (socially). Jesus grew into perfect maturity, as God intends for us as well.

If all dimensions of growth were necessary for Jesus, they are certainly necessary for us as well. We should have a sensible view of our bodies and keep them as healthy as possible for the Lord's work. We must grow in wisdom, which includes understanding what is happening in our world in the present and also being aware of our history—as a local community as well as a national and global community. We must also grow socially. We are supposed to learn how to love people and interact in a mature way, not bickering and squabbling like immature youngsters. We are, above all, supposed to develop spiritually. This aspect of maturity is what Paul addresses in 1 Corinthians 13.

Paul tells the Corinthians he can't treat them as adults but must treat them as children because he has to keep repeating the things he's already taught them. That's what children are like—you have to tell them again and again until they get it. Does God have to tell you things again and again? These baby Christians were like children, and Paul urges them to stop thinking like children with regard to doctrine and the gifts of the Holy Spirit. "In regard to evil be infants, but in your thinking be adults" (1 Corinthians 14:20). Are you a child where learning the rudimentary things of God is concerned? Then you need to grow up.

The Spirit of God grows us up. The Spirit's pure art makes us like Jesus in all dimensions of our humanity, and as far as I can remember (I am a teacher by trade), I never met a normal child who didn't want to grow up. Every child I know looks forward to celebrating his or her next birthday. I've never heard one say, "I want to stay the same age for another year." This sentiment is reserved for people who reach the age of forty or so and want to stop having birthdays!

So how long have you known Christ? Have you grown, and are you growing up in Christ? Paul is talking to the Philippians about spiritual maturity, but his words apply to all of us. He wants all who know Christ to want to be spiritually bigger than they are.

Paul gives us a clue about how to assess our spiritual maturity. For example, the first thing he says is that as believers mature and grow through the work of the Spirit in their lives, they should take "such a view of things" (Philippians 3:15). To what view does he refer? The illustration he has just given. He wants them to think maturely, as he does, about the whole purpose of life. He is looking back to his attitude of the "one thing I do" (3:13). He wants believers to focus all they are on the goal of finishing the race of faith for Christ and his kingdom. This attitude is a mature attitude. Is it yours? Is it mine?

We will know if we are growing in Christ if we are making church, ministry, and spiritual discipline a top priority. We'll know we are growing if we are putting spiritual things above material things—if we're praying about a career move, for example, and we find ourselves willing to seek out the right thing, even if it may not be the most profitable thing. We will know we are growing if we step out and offer to serve others in ways we haven't dared to try before, or if we start to mentor someone who needs guidance and a bit of spiritual tender loving care.

I remember a girl I had helped to get started in the Christian life, who then turned around and began to help her sister get started in the faith. When she began to help someone else instead of just receiving help herself, she showed real signs of maturity. You can often tell that a person is growing in Christ by their lifestyle and choices, by their goals, and by their overarching purpose to please God and finish well.

However, Paul was aware that some of his readers would not agree with him. He knew that many believed he took things to extremes. But Paul didn't consider this teaching about purpose in life to be an extreme; he considered it to be an attitude characteristic of the mature. "All of us who are mature should take this point of view," he says with confidence. And he adds words to this effect: "If you don't see it the way I do, the Spirit of God will convince you otherwise" (3:15).

A MODEL OF GROWTH
AND LEARNING

Paul is not being arrogant when he says, "Join with others in following my example" (Philippians 3:17). He is not saying that he has finished growing. We never finish growing. "I haven't attained," he tells us. "I am not fully grown, but my determination is to grow and grow and grow until my last breath." He is confident enough of his standing in Christ to say, "I am an example of this principle of maturity. I have cooperated with the Spirit's work in me, and I want you to do the same." And then he adds, "I am not the only good example to follow either. There are other mature people you should be taking note of." He advises his readers to look around and find a person to emulate—someone with this same mature attitude and unwavering passion for God.

Years ago, a friend of mine—a godly Christian woman—and I were talking about growing in Christ. I had been approached by a young woman who wanted me to mentor her. I talked it over with my friend, whom I considered to be wonderfully mature and one of my own models and mentors. "I don't know if I feel comfortable being an example," I told her. "I don't like putting myself on a pedestal."

"Well, Jill," she replied, "in the end we are only models of growth and learning." Hearing this released me to invest in the life of the young woman who had asked me to help her grow up into maturity. Look around you. You will find people who are mature in the faith. Join a Sunday school class or a Bible study and put yourself in touch with leaders in your community who have grown up to be godly people.

When I was a young Christian, a deacon from my church invited me to meet his wife, Mrs. Godden. I began making it a habit to stop by on the way home from work and have a cup of tea with this sweet lady. I never wanted to leave. We didn't talk theology but just talked about Jesus. I watched how she handled her children and how she and her husband interacted. I even watched how she ironed the clothes as we talked, and I wondered at her meticulous housekeeping skills. She amazed me. Everything she did, she explained, she did for Jesus. She was quiet but a lot of fun to be around, and I couldn't wait for my daily visits. She was a mature Christian woman, and I thank God for her and her influence in my life. Her two boys were great, and by meeting Christian kids in a Christian family, I was introduced to a whole new world.

Amazingly, I recently met one of those boys at a convention in the United Kingdom. I had lost touch with the family after marrying Stuart and moving away from Liverpool over fifty years ago. The boy had grown into a fine young man and has been a Baptist pastor now for many years. Here he was—at a convention for pastors and leaders, and I was a presenter at that event.

I sat down with him over a cup of tea and told him about the influence his mother had had in my life. He cried. I cried!

You don't have to look for Christian "stars." Look around you. Find a Mrs. Godden. And as Paul told his friends, "Take note of those [like Mrs. Godden] who live according to the pattern we gave you" (Philippians 3:17). But don't only look for an example to follow, a mentor from whom to learn. Grow up yourself and become a mentor for others.

Being a model of growth and learning presupposes that you share lessons from your own faith walk with others. It's good for us to be transparent. I suppose we could call this "the spiritual art of vulnerability." It's good for those who look to us to hear about both our failures and our victories. For example, it's all right to tell people that you struggle with worry and fear, even though a mature Christian is supposed to have overcome these things. Paul told the Philippians that they encouraged him in his struggles. "You are going through the same struggle you saw I had, and now hear that I still have," he tells them (1:30). This is admitting to the church that he has been discouraged because of all that has happened to him. His vulnerability makes him human and accessible to his friends; our vulnerability will make us human and accessible to others as well.

I have found that when I share the struggles I've had in the past, as well as the struggles of the present (advisedly, of course), people tell me, "When you shared that story, I realized that you are human just like me." Of course, if you only share the defeats and never the victories, then who is going to benefit from your example? I try to use language like Paul's: "I haven't attained, but I'm attaining. I'm determined to overcome this or that challenge in my life." By doing so, you invite dialogue, welcome people into your life experiences, and are able to help people grow up into maturity.

So by all means, look for a mentor. Pray about it. Ask God to show you the people you can look to. The mentor who can serve as a good example may be alive or they may be dead, but that's all right. Most of my early mentors were famous missionaries like Amy Carmichael, Gladys Aylward, Hudson Taylor, and C. T Studd. Some of these people were alive when I first came to faith, and some weren't. I read everything I could get my hands on about their lives and relationship with the Lord. These incredible people walked into my life and established a presence that molded my thinking of a world that must be won for Christ. They wrote of their relationship with God and their determination to know him better. They shared their disappointments in fellow missionaries. They talked of the dark nights of the soul, loneliness, and sickness with no doctor near to help. They let me sit in a corner of their lives—just as I sat in the corner of Mrs. Godden's kitchen—and watch them grow into maturity. I admired them and saw how they loved God, and I imitated their faith walk as best I could.

People who set my sails were ordinary people in my church circle, then missionaries and writers. They included C. S. Lewis, a professor at Cambridge during my training there; John Stott, rector of All Souls Church, Langham Place, in London; and "the Doctor," Martyn Lloyd-Jones, at Westminster Chapel. These mentors gripped my attention and my heart as I listened to them preach and pray. They had a life-changing influence on my spiritual journey.

I remember sitting in Westminster Chapel with other university students from Cambridge listening to the good Doctor pray before he preached. It took a good twenty minutes. I could hardly stop myself from jumping up at the end of his prayer and shouting out, "Don't stop. Please don't stop!" I had been taken into the heavenly throne room. Dr. Martyn Lloyd-Jones taught me in one sitting how to talk to the Father in heaven, and it changed my life. Right then and there I told God, "I want to know you like that." I didn't say that I wanted to pray that well—rather, that I wanted to know God like that. That was because the Doctor's prayer revealed how well he knew the Lord, and his prayer caused every person in that historic church to want to know God like that too. He mentored me in the art of prayer.

So don't pout if you don't have a wonderful mentor at present. Find one in biographies, mission archives, or church history. Just hang around these grown-up Christians, and let the mist of the mysteries of God rub off on you. Paul was able to say to people, "Watch me and imitate me." Don't you wish you could have been around at that time? What would it have been like to visit Paul in jail and observe how a mature Christian handled such affliction?

The young woman who led me to Christ mentored me. She was a relatively new believer herself, yet a mature one. One day she said, "You need to learn to pray."

"I don't know how," I answered.

"Shut your eyes and listen to me," she replied.

So I did. She prayed, and when she was finished, she opened her eyes and said, "Now *you* pray." I did my best as I imitated her. Since that day I've helped many others learn the rudiments of prayer in that same way.

But the rudiments aren't enough. We must grow up in our communication with God. We must ask the Spirit to teach us to be adult pray-ers. The Bible says that "we don't know what to ask for when we pray, but the Holy Spirit will help us in our infirmities and enable us to pray aright" (Romans 8:26–27, my translation).

It's God's pure spiritual art in our lives. Anyone can do it. Age makes no difference.

YOU CAN BE SPIRITUALLY OLD AND PHYSICALLY YOUNG, OR SPIRITUALLY YOUNG AND PHYSICALLY OLD

Paul understood that his readers would have different reactions to his challenge to be spiritually mature, and he declares that the evidence of spiritual maturity does not depend on age. Paul encourages a young Timothy not to "let anyone look down on you because you are young" (though he doesn't tell him how to stop others from looking down on him), but rather to be an example to old and young alike (1 Timothy 4:12). He is to teach both old and young "these things" (4:11). What things?

Timothy is to set an example for the believers "in speech, in life, in love, in faith and in purity" (4:12). Until Paul arrives, Timothy is instructed by his spiritual father and mentor to devote himself to "the public reading of Scripture, to preaching and to teaching" (4:13). He is not to neglect his gift (see 4:14). Here is a man young in years, yet old in spiritual wisdom. Conversely, we can be old in years and yet be children in understanding—infants in the faith. And, of course, we can be well up in years and be spiritually wise as well.

GOD PAINTS HIS PRETTIEST COLORS IN HIS LATEST SUNSETS

Having enjoyed many years of life myself, I am captivated by the examples of older people and their achievements. Not all are believers, yet they are all models to me. As I looked for old-timers who were still going strong in old age, I found the following:

- *Cornelius "Commodore" Vanderbilt*, the nineteenth-century American railroad magnate who built most of his railroads when he was seventy and earned hundreds of millions at an age when most men have retired.
- *Immanuel Kant*, the eighteenth-century German philosopher who wrote some of his greatest philosophical works when he was past the age of seventy.
- *Johann Wolfgang von Goethe*, the eighteenth-century German author and dramatist who wrote the second part of his famous tragedy *Faust* after he was eighty.
- *Victor Hugo*, the nineteenth-century French novelist who was still astounding the world with some of his finest writings after his eightieth birthday.
- *Alfred Lord Tennyson*, the nineteenth-century British poet laureate who was eighty-three when he wrote his famous poem "Crossing the Bar."
- *Michelangelo*, the Italian Renaissance painter and sculptor who was still producing masterpieces at the age of eighty.

What an encouragement for an older author and teacher like me!

Then, of course, we have biblical examples. Moses began his life's work at the age of eighty, and Caleb asks for his mountain—and rids it of giants and the like—also at eighty! The birth of Jesus was celebrated by Anna, who had been a widow for eighty-four years (see Luke 2:37 TNIV). Simeon, too, was elderly when he held the baby Jesus in his arms and prophesied in the temple about this Christ child who came to this earth to bring salvation (see Luke 2:25–35). All are examples of godly industry while life lasts and while sufficient health is given to run the race all the way to the finish line.

I am reminded of yet another old saint, General William Booth, cofounder with his wife, Catherine, of the Salvation Army. In his last days, Booth became blind. His son Bramwell visited him, and his father is reputed to have asked, "Is it true, Bramwell, that I will never see your face again?"

"It's true, father," Bramwell replied. After a while, William Booth said, "Well, I have served the Lord Jesus Christ all these years *with* my eyes; now I will serve him the rest of my life *without* them." What an example of finishing strong. Whether healthy or not! Sometimes God does indeed paint his prettiest colors in his latest sunsets.

MARKS OF MATURITY

So how does the Spirit work his art of Christlikeness into our lives? Not without our cooperation. Sorry, it's that little word again — "discipline." The Spirit's part is to help us to be obedient to do his work, and ours is to order our lives and practice the spiritual disciplines. But how?

As it is in the physical realm so it is in the spiritual: we cannot grow unless we eat. "Like newborn babies, crave pure spiritual milk," says the apostle Peter, writing to the Jews scattered in Asia, "so that by it you may grow up in your salvation, now that you have tasted that the Lord is good" (1 Peter 2:2–3). If human babies must eat to grow, then so must spiritual babies. As we absorb, read, highlight, learn, and inwardly digest the Scriptures, we become mature believers and good examples to others. Get a Bible that has type large enough for comfortable reading, and read a little every day—twice a day if you can, morning and evening. Sit quietly and think about what you've read. Ask some questions and figure out the answers. Apply the lessons, and then put them into practice.

That's where you start. Then begin to study the Bible more than you do now. Go deeper. This is different from simply reading it and asking questions about the text. Get a layperson's commentary from a Christian bookstore and use it to study a book or an epistle. Take notes as you go along. Apply the lessons learned from it. As you craved milk when you were first came to faith in Jesus, crave more than milk now. Crave solid food. That's what grown-ups eat. You can often find out how mature or immature you are by the spiritual diet you have chosen. What spiritual food have you had this week? Did you enjoy a good meal every day, or did you starve all week and have all your meals on Sunday? That's what a lot of churchgoers do.

You can gauge your maturity by the way people look to you as an example. Is your life worth imitating when it comes to Bible knowledge? Do people ask you to show them how to know their Bible like you do?

We should be able to say, as Paul could say to the Corinthians, "In Christ Jesus I became your father through the gospel. Therefore I urge you to imitate me" (1 Corinthians 4:15b–16). He then tells them that he is sending Timothy to them, who will remind them of Paul's way of life, "which agrees with what I teach everywhere in every church" (4:17).

Does our way of life agree with what we teach? Are we consistent in lifestyle with our profession as Christians? Are we getting our life instructions from God's Word and being obedient to these directions? Can we help others to do the same?

DO WE HANDLE OUR DIFFERENCES LIKE "BIG PEOPLE," AND DO WE LOVE THE PEOPLE WITH WHOM WE DIFFER?

One of the most significant signs of the spiritual art of maturity is how well we handle our differences. Do we handle our differences Christianly? Is there a spirit of competition in our church, and are we caught up in it? Paul told the Corinthians he could not address their quarrels maturely, because they were like a bunch of kids fighting over their favorite preacher. "I gave you milk, not solid food, for you were not yet ready for it," Paul tells them (1 Corinthians 3:2). You cannot grow into spiritual maturity while you are dividing the church and taking sides.

Another sign that you are cooperating with God is a growing love for people—a love that transcends all barriers, a love that loves those you don't even like. And even a love for the lost, both outside and inside the church. Paul talks with concern and compassion about some people who are "enemies of the cross of Christ" (Philippians 3:18). It's not immediately clear who these people are. Paul observes, "Their destiny is destruction, their god is their stomach, and their glory is in their shame. Their mind is on earthly things" (3:19). They could be libertines who were in some way connected with the church—a group of people who believed that once they had become followers of Christ, they were free from all moral constraint. It didn't matter what they did; they were forgiven anyway.

The phrase "their god is their stomach" really speaks of more than gluttony and includes sensual indulgence as well. Some think that Paul is talking about Judaizers, who want to heap all sorts of laws and restrictions on new believers. However, these words of Paul don't seem to be describing Judaizers, because these "enemies of the cross" are described in verse 19 as gluttons and materially minded people.

THE MATURE CARE DEEPLY ABOUT LOST PEOPLE

One way or another, Paul is in tears as he talks about these people (3:18). It breaks his heart to see these things happening. He loves the sinner and hates the sin. Do we? Or do we rebuke the sinner and separate our hearts and our selves from their dilemmas? "They are lost," says Paul. Do we care—*really care*—about lost people? Be honest. Would you rather bury yourself among Christians than spend time trying to make friends and establish contacts so that in the end they can come to know the Lord Jesus? The answer to this question will show you if you've grown up yet.

If we really love people with the love of Christ, we will care about people who live like the devil and think that they will get away with it. We know that isn't true. "Their destiny is destruction," says Paul (3:19). Have we tried to get to them and warn them of what will become of their philosophy?

I've talked to some people who think that being a Christian surely means that God will wipe dry every tear and keep them in a perpetual state of giddy happiness, no matter what the state of the world around them and the spiritual state of people's souls might be. This is childish thinking. It's immature. If this is what is happening in your life at present, you haven't yet grown up in Christ. Jesus himself wept over a people who rejected their Messiah and were headed for eternal destruction (see Luke 19:41–44). Did this mean that Jesus was not mature because he was not happy all the time? Sharing the pain Jesus feels for the lost is a grown-up thing to do. Jesus was the supreme example, of course, but Paul also serves an example of one who cried many tears for those who were lost and alienated from God.

In Acts 20, Paul says good-bye to the Ephesian elders (verse 37). They will never see him again, and they shed many tears. Paul reminds them he lived with them for three years, never ceasing to warn them that, after his death, wolves would get among the sheep and wreak spiritual havoc (20:31). They would ruin the faith of some and turn off others to the faith. He says, "Remember that for three years I never stopped warning each of you night and day with tears." Paul spent three years crying over their spiritual well-being! How many years have we spent weeping over the immaturity of believers in our churches?

So Paul reveals his heart—his broken heart. It only happens to mature people. To cry for the lost as well as the found is the Spirit's art. To be Christlike in this sense—caring deeply for those bound for destruction and to weep over the Christians in danger of being led astray, even by some "from your own number" who will "distort the truth" (20:30)—shows that you have stopped thinking about yourself first and started caring about others first. This cry of the soul is the Spirit's art.

As I write this chapter, I think of people who cause me grave concern. I have cried for, prayed for, and worried about them. I don't like to be like this. I'd rather be happy. I tend to be far too fond of myself to open myself up to more tears. But I can't bring myself to pray, "Lord, make it so I don't care so much." And as I reflect on it, I'm glad I can't pray that. I guess I'm growing up. It's about time! I care so deeply that I am driven to continue to pray and to continue to warn those I love until I take my final breath.

Paul sums up his insights on being an example of a mature, caring, loving, growing person by reminding his readers that they belong to a king and a country whose main characteristic is that of a heavenly, not earthly, perspective. "Our citizenship is in heaven," he says (Philippians 3:20). Once we know the King of the kingdom and start to follow him home, we know we are citizens of heaven. We play by new rules, meet new friends, march to the beat of a new drum, and are proud to be a citizen of the "High Countries."

I hold two passports—European and American. When I became a United States citizen, I swore to abide by this country's rules, to honor the government, and to try to be a productive citizen. That meant learning to live in a new culture, following new rules and regulations, and developing a new way of life. Last year was the tipping point when I realized that I had lived as long in the United States as I had in the United Kingdom. I feel like a woman with my feet firmly planted in the mid-Atlantic. I enjoy the joys of America and embrace the responsibilities and privileges of my citizenship as well.

The great thing about becoming a citizen of heaven is that I embrace the grace, privileges, and responsibilities of this great honor too. I really hold three passports—European, American, and my heavenly one.

Being citizens of heaven means that one day we will be fully mature, for we will see him face-to-face, and when we see him, "we shall be like him" (1 John 3:2). Then there will be no more tears and no more pain. God will wipe away every tear from our eyes (Revelation 7:17; 21:4). What a day that will be! All wrongs will be righted, all sicknesses healed, all hatred turned to love— and reconciliation will be complete. All things will be brought under his control (see Philippians 3:21). I can't wait! Like Paul, I eagerly await Christ's glorious appearing (see 3:20).

"LASH UP AND STOW, BOYS; THE BOSS MAY COME TODAY."

Stuart and I were recently privileged to go to Antarctica. We were with some friends on an adventure ship and followed the story of Ernest Henry Shackleton, the famous British explorer who spent his life trying to be the first to get to the South Pole. He didn't succeed, but that didn't stop him trying to get there anyway, over and over again. With us was a British history professor from Cambridge University, who kept us enthralled with the story of vision, leadership, determination, courage, persistence, and death that is the Shackleton story.

Each day we got into small boats called Zodiacs and made wet landings on land masses or ice floes. One day we landed on Elephant Island, a part of Antarctica where Shackleton's ship, *Endurance*, was crushed in the ice and sank. He and his men began their biggest adventure yet—surviving one of the world's most hostile environments. Here Shackleton left twenty-two of his men, with Frank Wild in charge, while he and five men left in a boat to go for help.

As we stood on Elephant Island, I tried to imagine what it must have been like to be one of those left behind—huddled under an upturned lifeboat, wondering if "the boss" (as they called Shackleton) had died at sea, and if that would also be their destiny.

Wild was a conservationist, so he allowed his men to kill only as many penguins as they needed each day to survive. What he couldn't know was that the birds would all leave in one night as part of their annual seasonal migration. Hungry, exhausted, and frightened, the men began to despair.

In an effort to keep their spirits up, Wild woke the twenty-two men early each day with the words, "Lash up and stow, boys;

the boss may come today." Day after anxious day they did just that, and then they settled down on that incredible and formidable Antarctic ice to peer out from under their upturned boat and to watch for the boss. A few days after the penguins left, Shackleton returned to save them. In the end, every man on Elephant Island survived.

Sometimes I imagine myself under a lifeboat on earth—a most inhospitable place—peering out at a formidable landscape, waiting hopefully and watching for my Savior to appear. "Surely he will come and save us!" I whisper. Paul exhorts us poor earthly mariners to eagerly await a Savior from heaven—he will come and will not delay. Even so, come, Lord Jesus!

QUESTIONS FOR REFLECTION
AND DISCUSSION

1. Read Philippians 3:15–21. If you had to choose one verse from this section to memorize, which would it be, and why?

2. Paul is talking about the art of spiritual maturity. Based on what you see in Philippians 3, how would you define this art?

3. How long have you known Christ? Would you consider yourself to be mature?

4. Paul wants disciples of Jesus to want to be spiritually "bigger" than they are right now—to be ambitious, like he was. What can we do to help others to grow in their faith? How can we be mentors to others?

5. Paul tells Timothy he is to "set an example for the believers in speech, in life, in love, in faith and in purity" (1 Timothy 4:12). Which of these mature traits do you need to work on? What's one step you could take within the next twenty-four hours?

6. Describe someone who has been an example to you. In what specific way did they help you to grow?

7. What are some of the marks of real spiritual maturity?

8. What do you think about weeping for the lost?

9. Does maturity have anything to do with age?

THOUGHTS FOR PRAYER

Pray for

- lost people,
- found people,
- mentors who have helped you in the past, and
- yourself and your family.

CHAPTER 7

the spiritual art of
serenity

I have learned the secret of being content
in any and every situation.
Philippians 4:12

Biblical peace is the Spirit's art in our troubled hearts. We end Paul's letter where we began. Paul, chained to what most of us would say were impossible circumstances, sings a song and dispenses blessings. He is content and at peace. Contentment, you remember, is a learned art, so we can learn the principles of faith that must be put into practice in order to live in a peaceful place. The spiritual art of serenity is an inner thing; it comes from the heart. It is perhaps the most sought-after art of all. Who doesn't want to be serene in the midst of chaos? The dictionary defines "serenity" as "tranquillity," "calmness," "an undisturbed state." God's Word defines it as biblical "peace."

Joy is faith dancing; peace is faith resting. Faith in a God who doesn't make mistakes, who has the whole world in his hands—including my worried world—releases us to laugh at dark days and to dance in the rain. The joy is in Jesus. Where can we find joy in life itself with all its drama and pain? We find it in God.

In Philippians 4, Paul returns to one of his key themes: "Rejoice in the Lord always" (4:4). *The Message* renders it, "Celebrate

God all day, every day. I mean, *revel* in him!" What a wonderful paraphrase! It is when we revel in God that we set our minds in the right direction. Whatever our circumstances, we need to do whatever it takes to enjoy God. All day, every day. Good days and bad days, bright days and dark days. Whether in prison or free, we need to learn how to sing our pain away.

Practicing the art of incorrigible thankfulness and praise sends worry tiptoeing out the backdoor of our lives. When you feel a worry coming on, sing a song—anything with the name of Jesus in it. Revel in him!

Peace is faith resting in the fact that God will carry our worries for us. Faith counts on it. It is our soul saying, "I will trust and not be afraid" (Isaiah 12:2), and, "Though the mountains fall down and my world disintegrates, *I* won't fall down and disintegrate, for I am banking on a God who is my refuge and strength, my Rock and my Redeemer" (Psalm 46:1–2; 19:14, my translation). The promise of a trustworthy God is this: "He will keep us in perfect peace if our minds are stayed on him—because we trust him" (Isaiah 26:3, my translation).

Paul's letter to the Philippians just gets better and better. It ends on such a high note. How can there be more and more things to rejoice about in situations in which there are more and more things to be concerned about? Paul, who had everything in the world to worry about, says to people who have a whole lot less to worry about than he did, "Take it from me; you don't need to worry about anything." It's not a question of things that we worry about disappearing off the radar screen, but rather a question of who is going to do the worrying about these things.

"Are there worrisome things around me?" asks the apostle Paul. "Oh, yes—like the trial I'm facing for my life, the care of all the churches I've planted, people I love who are dying for their faith in Jesus, old age and sickness, and sorrow upon sorrow. But I'm resting. I have perfect peace, because I have put it all on God's cosmic shoulders, and he is carrying the crushing weight for me." Such tranquillity of thought and mind is priceless.

PUT IT IN MY BACKPACK

A while ago, Stuart and I went bird-watching in Wisconsin, one of our favorite things to do. We took a few days off to celebrate my birthday (yes, I actually still have them once a year). We walked the trails in the beautiful forests of our state. One morning, Stuart shouldered his backpack that was loaded with water, maps, binoculars, a camera, and so on. I decided I would just carry my binoculars and camera and not deal with the extra weight of a backpack. We set off on a glorious morning—and oh, oh, oh, what a thrill! To be alone with each other and with God and his incredible handiwork, and to walk and walk and walk. Joy!

After lunch, we set off again, and this time the trail was more isolated and hilly. By now I had gathered a few items along the way, and my hands were full. My heavy binoculars got heavier, and the bundles I carried felt cumbersome. I was dragging.

The trail was very narrow, and we couldn't walk side by side so I walked behind my man and looked at his strong, straight shoulders ahead of me on which his quite full backpack was setting. Suddenly, as though sensing my fatigue, he turned around, smiled at me gently, and said, "Jill, put it all in my backpack."

I stood quite still as the impact of the offer sank in. In addition to the paraphernalia of the birder, I also carried an unseen burden of worry along with me that day. I took all of my stuff and put it in Stuart's backpack. Then we continued to walk the trails. Oh, the freedom!

"Why don't you put it all in my backpack, Jill?" the Lord whispered to my heavy heart as we walked. Though my hands were empty, my heart was still loaded down with worry. And there, walking along that beautiful Wisconsin trail, I transferred another load of stuff. It didn't mean I no longer had a burden; it meant that God carried it instead of me. What a difference! The problem hadn't gone away, but God's strong, eternal shoulders bore the weight of it for me. I rejoiced! Joy is faith dancing, and peace is faith resting.

Are you walking with a heavy weight on your heart? A worry so grievous it crushes you and spoils the day? Put it in God's backpack. Then you'll not only be conscious of the fact you don't walk the trail alone, but you will find yourself strangely lightened in spirit—and, yes, then your spirit rests, tranquillity reigns, and all is well.

Another word for *peace* is "serenity"—the "tranquillity of order," as Saint Augustine called it.* When things are not the way things ought to be, God's peace disappears. Perfect peace or contentment can be ours as God puts our soul back in order inside of us, even though chaos reigns outside of us.

Paul knew that he was in the school of life, with all of its problems, cooperating with the Spirit of God and learning tranquillity on a daily basis. "I have learned to be content," he tells his friends. Each day as he awoke from a cramped position on his hard bed, Paul asked God for his waking thought. Next came a psalm or spiritual song such as, "This is the day the LORD has made; let us rejoice and be glad in it" (Psalm 118:24). And he would be glad and light of heart. "I will be glad," he said. "I will be glad, even when everything inside of me is screaming, 'I won't. I can't. Why should I? It's unfair to expect me to.'"

---

*Augustine, *The City of God* (public domain, book 19, chapter 13).

The strange thing is that it takes work to rest in faith like this. Work and faith sound almost like an oxymoron, don't they? I have this framed saying sitting on my kitchen table:

> *Bear not a single care thyself,*
> *One is too much for thee;*
> *The work is mine, yes, mine alone,*
> *Thy work to rest in me.*

The Spirit's work is to provide his serenity in the midst of a storm; our work is to stop trying to manufacture it ourselves and to be at peace, to rest—and that, of course, is a spiritual art. I have never met anyone who doesn't want to be at peace with themselves, others, and the world around them. Isn't this true for us too—ordinary, run-of-the-mill human beings that we are? So how does it work? Is it a matter of peace at any price? If not, what is the price we must pay to cooperate with the Spirit and to have him write his language on our hearts?

PEACE IN THE BANK

First, God wants us to know that we have "peace in the bank" if we have Jesus. He is our peace. When the Prince of Peace is given the keys of the kingdom of our hearts, he brings us peace—wealth to be drawn on as needed. The peace of God can be appropriated. When one is a Christian, there are deposits of peace made over to us in Christ. When trouble hits, in whatever form, say to yourself, "For this we have Jesus." Remember, Paul said, "To live is Christ" (Philippians 1:21). He is our life, and he is also our peace (see Ephesians 2:14).

If people are enjoying the peace of Christ—a peace with God that brings peace with others, and thus our own peace of mind—you can tell it by their words. Listen to the conversations around you in an airport, in a store, or at an athletic event. Tune in to the conversations among the kids at the swimming pool, in the classroom, or even at church. How much of this chatter is about worries and concerns, fears and phobias? How much is about faith, peace, and contentment?

Stuart and I spoke at a conference for senior adults not long ago. There were over four hundred people there, and we had a great time. We spent each mealtime with these dear Christian folk who are in the autumn and winter seasons of their lives, and we listened to them and encouraged them. Concerns about their churches were high on the list of topics of conversation, and they shared that they sometimes felt marginalized and unneeded. But mostly the conversation seemed to revolve around their families. They worried about their children and their grandchildren. "What a world we live in!" they lamented. "So different from the world in which we were raised." We agreed. Young families have to battle things we didn't. They have so much more lined up against them. Stuart and I spent considerable time worrying with them about "the bad new days" while lauding "the good old days." Of course, that's what old folks like us do! We tend to have selective memories and forget the bad things about the good old days and then keep worrying about the bad new days.

Among other things, I spoke at this conference about passing on one's faith to the next generation. Tears flowed, and those sweet grandparents wept over divorced children and over grandchildren far away from the Lord. They spent hours praying for them. "We feel helpless," they said. And, of course, that's what grandparents do feel so often. Stuart and I have thirteen grandchildren, and

I can tell you all about feeling helpless and out of control. (Of course, you really are out of control when you are a parent, but you just won't admit it!) When you're out of control, there is one thing you *can* do, however—worry. Then at least you feel you're doing something about the situation. But does it help? Worry, I have discovered, empties today of its strength and, of course, does nothing about tomorrow or yesterday. The bottom line is that the Lord has told us not to waste our energy worrying. There's one good thing about getting older—the only good thing, as far as I can tell: the older you get, the more you have to worry about, so the more practice God gives you in learning to let his peace control your life.

DON'T WORRY ABOUT ANYTHING

Paul says we are not to worry about *anything* (see Philippians 4:6). I have been a worrier since childhood. It may well have something to do with World War II, but my personality leans in that negative direction as well. When I became a Christian, I was confronted with doing something about my constant worrying. So I set about finding out what the Bible said about my chronic anxiety. I remember reading Philippians for the first time. There it was: "Do not be anxious about anything."

I had been introduced to a very simple method of Bible reading. With three colored pencils in hand, I searched for promises, commands, and warnings in the text. I marked them in different colors. So when I found myself reading, "Do not be anxious about anything," I marked it in blue because it was the color I used for commands to obey. I had been told not to worry. To obey his commands was to please God; to disobey his commands was to grieve him. Worry now became a sin!

It's important to draw a distinction here. There is worry, and then there is concern. Concern is a given for a Christian. Paul was concerned, and Timothy was concerned. Concern is "right" worry. In fact, in chapter 2 Paul tells the Philippian Christians that he had no one like Timothy, who had such heart concern for them (see verse 20). But concern isn't self-directed or self-destructive. It looks for a way to relieve other people's worries and troubles, not add to them. And it is a "worry" that turns itself into prayers.

Worry that is forbidden to the believer is that grinding, blinding obsession that slays your spirit, destroys your appetite, and kills your hope. It is the worry that swamps you and makes you gasp so you can hardly breathe. It is an emotional flu that never gets better.

But a worry that is turned into a positive heart concern—one that looks for solutions and makes us more sensitive to people's heart needs—is what God wants us to have. In Philippians you can't help but see Paul's heart concern at the deepest level for his friends. But he doesn't allow the problems of those he loves to dictate every waking moment of his life, intrude on his other relationships, or drag him down into depression. He doesn't let it obsess him or paralyze him. To do that, he knows, is wrong.

JESUS HAS FORBIDDEN ME TO WORRY

It really helps me to know that anxiety is forbidden. "Do not let your hearts be troubled" (John 14:1), counseled Jesus. I have noticed that worry and fear are near allies. Jesus tells us not to let worry dominate our lives. Don't let it? That means we can do something to stop it—and that something is *trust*. The act of not letting worry dominate us but rather letting the peace of God dominate us is a learned art—a spiritual art.

Fearing for your life is forbidden by Jesus. In Matthew 6:27, Jesus asks, "Who of you by worrying can add a single hour to his life?" You can go to the grave having worried about all the days you weren't going to live and have the opportunity to worry about! In fact, some of us will go to the grave having worried about keeping ourselves alive until the moment comes. It's such a freeing thing to trust God with that. Put it in his backpack.

To the people of his day—and to us today—Jesus declared, "Give your entire attention to what God is doing right now, and don't get worked up about what may or may not happen tomorrow. God will help you deal with whatever hard things come up when the time comes" (Matthew 6:34 MSG). If you trust, you do not worry; if you worry, you do not trust. Ask the Lord for the grace to trust him.

When Stuart and I travel, particularly in England, we love to wander through English graveyards. Epitaphs are a source of interest and wonder to us. Just a line or two on a gravestone sets you wondering why that sentence was chosen to summarize the life of the one in the grave. Here are a couple of my favorites: "Here lies a man who went out of the world without ever knowing why he came into it!" That's sad. And another: "Here lies the Reverend So-and-So, who served God without enthusiasm"—a Puritan's grave! I have often wondered about my own gravestone. I don't want someone to sum up my life with, "Here lies Jill Briscoe, who worried herself to death."

We know that worry is a precursor of many physical problems. It is also evidence of all sorts of spiritual problems. For whatever is a lack of faith is sin. I would like to have my epitaph read, "Here lies Jill Briscoe, who overcame worry and fear with faith and helped others to do the same." I'm working on making this statement true in my life.

WORRY DISTRACTS US
FROM THE ESSENTIALS

The Greek word used for the bad sort of worry is *merimnaō*—the anxiety that obsesses. It means "to be distracted," "to have a divided mind." And isn't that just what worry does? It divides your mind and distracts you from everything else going on around you. I call it the "Martha, Martha" syndrome.

Do you remember the story as recorded by Luke? Eugene Peterson renders it this way:

> As they continued their travel, Jesus entered a village. A woman by the name of Martha welcomed him and made him feel quite at home. She had a sister, Mary, who sat before the Master, hanging on every word he said. But Martha was pulled away by all she had to do in the kitchen. Later, she stepped in, interrupting them. "Master, don't you care that my sister has abandoned the kitchen to me? Tell her to lend me a hand."
>
> The Master said, "Martha, dear Martha, you're fussing far too much and getting yourself worked up over nothing. One thing only is essential, and Mary has chosen it—it's the main course, and won't be taken from her."
>
> *Luke 10:38–41 MSG*

Worry distracted Martha from the essentials. Worry made her critical of her sister and of Jesus too. Worry takes our eyes off Jesus and puts them on the things that cause our worry. Worry divides the mind and distresses the spirit. Martha had legitimate worries, but they became illegitimate when she allowed them to divide her mind and distract her from the most essential thing.

The problem with worry is that it is infectious. It spreads itself around, and others catch the worry germ. When David, our firstborn, was a toddler, he was late in talking. It could be that his mother didn't let him get a word in edgewise, or just that he was one of those late bloomers. Anyway, I well remember the first words he uttered. I had been told that I needed to write down my children's first words, and so I flew for my pencil to record the momentous utterance. Then I froze. David's first words were, "Oh, dear!" Now then, to whom had he been listening all day? His mother! Worry is infectious. Martha was contaminated with it as she began complaining and spreading her germs all over the room. Don't do it. Tackle it head-on. Get on your knees and say, "Lord, forgive me. Teach me how to trust you."

As we reflect again on the apostle Paul, we know that he had lots of legitimate things to be worried about. He was in chains — his freedom taken away — and things were out of control. If he had been making a list about all the things to worry about, it would have been a long list. It may have looked something like this:

- I am worried about the fledgling church in Philippi and the churches in other places as well.
- I am worried about competition among believers — the comparisons and criticism that can be so rampant.
- I am worried about two dear strong women — my fellow workers who have had a falling-out with each other.
- I am worried about Epaphroditus's health.
- I am worried about my own health.
- I am worried about my upcoming trial and possible death sentence.

Maybe Paul made a list, but if he did, he put it in God's backpack and let the strong shoulders of the Lord carry all his anxiety for him. Paul's mind was not divided; nor did he allow himself to be consumed with worry about himself and those he loved.

What would *your* list look like? Are you chained to a marriage that is less than all it should be? Have you lost your job—or does your job feel like a dead end? Maybe children who don't know the Lord would be on your list. Or parents—or even a spouse or good friends—who don't know the Lord. It could be that you are frightened about the future—or even about whether the basic needs of your family can be met. Above all, there is the growing worry about safety and security in an age of frightening violence and uncertainties.

Would your list be long? Mine would. Actually, most of us don't need to make a list on paper, because it is engraved on our minds. And that's part of the problem, but it's also where the solution starts. We have to get ahold of our minds. It is in the mind that we do our part, and God then responds to our part and does his, as we'll see in the closing section of Philippians.

Let me walk you through Paul's formula for winning the worry war. It's an art, of course, and one well worth mastering.

PRAYER IS WHERE YOU START

Avoid the temptation to say, "But I can't seem to pray when I'm worried." Prayer is simply verbalizing your worry to God. You can verbalize your worries out loud or silently, for God's ears are not too dull to hear (see Isaiah 59:1). Replace worry with prayer. "Instead of worrying, pray," says Paul (Philippians 4:6 MSG). Prayer combats worry by building trust.

There are all sorts of ways of verbalizing your concerns to God. A few are mentioned in Philippians 4. In fact, there is a list: prayer, petition, requests, thanksgiving.

Prayer is essentially worshipful conversation with God. *Petition* refers to a prayer containing a sense of need. *Requests* are direct appeals for God's help for specific needs. When all this is done, wrap your bundle of prayers in a blanket of *thanksgiving* and deliver it to the throne and leave it there. Or if we return to my hiking experience, put it in God's backpack. As you let go of it all, find something to thank God for in the situation, no matter how bad it is.

The Message says, "Let petitions and praises shape your worries into prayers" (4:6). I love that. Take that old worry by the scruff of the neck and shape it into a prayer. Worry hates that. But that's how a wrong worry becomes a right worry — turning it into a godly concern and becoming an intercession. Try it!

PRAYER CHANGES THINGS SOMETIMES, BUT PRAYER CHANGES *YOU* ALWAYS

A common idea is that trusting God with our anxieties will make them disappear. Here's what the thought process typically sounds like:

- If I pray hard enough, the sickness will be healed.
- If I pray long enough, my spouse will come back to me.
- If I pray with more faith, the threat will go away.
- If I pray with real faith, the situation will change overnight.

God may well decide to work this way. So, by all means, ask — requests are supposed to be specific — but prayer itself is so much more than specific requests. Prayer is just being with God, enjoying him, and absorbing his will for you. Prayer isn't just something you *do*; it's somewhere you go to experience the presence of God. And *that* is a spiritual art.

Prayer, of course, is listening to God as well as talking to him. Listening is not always the thing we want to do, is it? We may be afraid that if we listen, we will hear him say no, or maybe he'll tell us to wait, and we're not willing to hear either of those answers.

Prayer is where God may well say, "This illness will not be healed"—as the Lord told Paul when the apostle asked that his thorn in the flesh be removed (see 2 Corinthians 12:7–10). Or God may say, "The danger will be ever present"—for example, if you live in a war-torn area or in "tornado alley." As we walk and talk with the Lord in the cool of the day, the unacceptable becomes acceptable. The cause of concern doesn't necessarily immediately disappear, but the worry over it can. Then, after telling God, "Your will be done," the prayers of petition can be prayed for endurance and strength. God is always going to answer such requests, as he did for Paul in the case of his thorn in the flesh. "My grace is sufficient for you, for my power is made perfect in weakness," the Lord said (2 Corinthians 12:9). Prayer brings you close to God so you can hear him saying, "This is the good way; walk in it" (Jeremiah 6:16, my translation). Prayer gives you the opportunity to accept the worrisome situation but to lay down the worry itself.

So the cause of concern may still be out there after an intense season of prayer. The situation may not be one whit different, but your mind-set has changed. You look at the concern in a totally different way. It's like going to the optometrist and getting glasses for the first time and realizing that you were virtually blind to things and didn't even know it. Now you can see to drive and to avoid the obstacles you could vaguely see and were afraid of. So prayer changes things—sometimes—but prayer changes *you* always.

Paul says that we are to pray about our worries with thanksgiving: "In everything, by prayer and petition, with thanksgiving, present your requests to God" (Philippians 4:6). What does he mean? Thank God for the worries? No. Thank God for who he is in the midst of the worries. Thank God for his strong eternal shoulders that are perfectly capable of carrying all the burdens of worry in the world—yours included.

Paul shows us how to do this. In fact, he reminds us of his own example when he says, "Whatever you have learned or received or heard from me, or seen in me—put it into practice. And the God of peace will be with you" (4:9). Paul's prayers are great places to learn how to pray. Begin by studying these, and you will find your prayer life changing dramatically. Listen to Paul pray, and then follow his lead.

The first thing we find Paul doing in Philippians 1 is praying for others. He prays about the things that have happened to him, especially those situations that have provided encouragement to the church. For this he gives thanks. He finds something to give thanks for—even in the tough situation in which he finds himself.

Pause right now and bring to mind a difficult situation you face. What can you find to thank God for in this instance? It may take a little time, but work at it. It's a spiritual art. When you've thought of something, just tell God, "Thank you." Go on, say it right now. Good. Keep practicing this all day long.

One of our friends was recently diagnosed with cancer. Her entire life changed in an instant. Prayers were and are still offered for her healing and will be until God's final, "No. I have something better for her in mind." Although her health is going downhill, our friend is going uphill. As she puts it, she isn't busy dying of cancer; she's busy living with cancer. The cancer hasn't gone away, and we don't know if it will. But she lets God worry about all of that and engages in a vibrant full-time ministry as her strength allows. She is an inspiration to all who are privileged to know her.

What has happened to her has been used to spread the gospel far and wide. She is chained to cancer at the moment, but her chains are chains of blessing, and she is incorrigibly cheerful and thankful. Each time I'm with her she is telling me something she is thankful about. She shapes her worries into prayers and wraps them in thanksgiving, and God is evidenced in the serenity that is hers.

It takes discipline to practice this attitude. It's an art—a spiritual art—to diligently look for something to thank God for. You need to focus. You need to "mind your mind" and not allow it to be distracted. Paul talks about setting your mind to do this work (see Philippians 4:8). Our part is to do this "mind work." Paul found something in his circumstances for which to give thanks, however grim the circumstances were. He occupied his mind with Godward thoughts. He tells us to program our minds with true, noble, right, pure, lovely, admirable, excellent, and praiseworthy things (4:8). Then, he says, "The God of peace will be with you" (4:9). When praise and positive thoughts go hand in hand, you discover something to praise God for—even from a dirty prison cell. Remember, serenity is a spiritual art.

When sisters Betsy and Corrie ten Boom were arrested by the Nazis for harboring Jews, they were sent to the infamous Ravensbrück concentration camp for women. On arrival, they were assigned to a smelly barracks crawling with fleas. Although they hated the pests, Betsy said, "Corrie, we must thank God for the fleas," and she proceeded to do so. Corrie had a harder time understanding how anyone could give thanks for anything as wretched as fleas. As time went on, however, Betsy and Corrie were surprised to find how openly they could hold Bible study and prayer times in the barracks without interference from the guards. They later discovered that the guards refused to enter the barracks because of the fleas. While it had taken Corrie a little while to follow Betsy's lead, she managed to do it and had learned, she said, to find many things to thank God for—even in the Ravensbrück concentration camp!

Paul tells us that the first thing to do when worries arise is *pray*. It shouldn't be the last response to a crisis but rather the first. And pray *with thanksgiving* before you "feel" like it. Feelings follow faith. Worry hates to hear you praying, but it particularly hates to hear you praying with thanksgiving. Worry hates praise. Music makes worry squirm.

I have found out a simple thing: you can't worry and pray at the same time. Try it! "Instead of worrying, pray"—and pray with thanksgiving (4:6). I love the paraphrase from *The Message*:

> Let petitions and praises shape your worries into prayers, letting
> God know your concerns. Before you know it, a sense of God's
> wholeness, everything coming together for good, will come
> and settle you down. It's wonderful what happens when Christ
> displaces worry at the center of your life.
>
> *Philippians 4:6–7 MSG*

The peace of God is ultimate spiritual contentment. It's a learned art to let this peace settle your worried heart.

It takes the Spirit to scatter his serenity around your heart. He cannot do it if you don't ask him to. Give him permission to move in and settle your restless, frantic, worried heart.

BIBLICAL SERENITY IS NOT THE ABSENCE OF CONFLICT

Biblical serenity is peace while the conflict is raging. It doesn't happen in a vacuum. When Jesus and the disciples were in the middle of the Sea of Galilee in a raging storm, the worry and fear of the disciples were understandable (see Mark 4:35–41). But Jesus didn't understand it. *He* was in the boat. He had the seat of honor reserved for the honored guest. Didn't they get it? If Jesus was in the boat, it didn't really matter whether they lived or died. Either way, they lived! He was asleep on a cushion in the back of the boat when the storm broke loose. He slept through it! How could he do that? Because he believed that his heavenly Father would carry his worries and cares. That he wouldn't go to heaven one minute before his hour came. Jesus slept! He believed that the God who "watches over Israel will neither slumber nor sleep" (Psalm 121:4), so he reckoned that there was no point in both of them staying awake.

GOD DOES THE GUARDING

When we refuse to worry about anything and commit to pray about everything, when we thank God for his dear and abiding self inside our hearts, then, Paul says, "the peace of God, which transcends all understanding, will guard your hearts and your minds in Christ Jesus" (Philippians 4:7).

The word "guard" brings into focus the image of a stronghold. God puts a garrison of soldiers around our hearts to face the enemy that besieges us. How does it happen? It happens when we respond to fear with faith, and to worry with worship. It happens when we are deep in God's Word on a daily basis, hiding verses of promise away for a rainy day.

One of my rainy days was August 10, 2006, flying into London's Heathrow Airport. Scotland Yard had just arrested a number of people suspected of trying to bomb planes scheduled to fly between London and New York, and we were about to land in the middle of a terrorist alert. There was an international emergency!

Was I safe — high in the sky over the Atlantic Ocean — when trouble came? I might or might not be safe in the airplane, but I was safe in God's arms. Running to him internally, I cast my fear and anxiety on him. In fact, I hurled it. That is what Scripture tells us to do: "Cast all your anxiety on him, because he cares for you" (1 Peter 5:7).

God was there, of course. My beating heart returned to its (almost) normal rate. There was peace. I looked around at the strangers near me. Did they know the Lord? Were they in turmoil? I knew that God could show them the peace in my heart. Over the next two weeks in the United Kingdom, first with four hundred African women (some were recent immigrants but most had been born there), and then with church leaders from all over the country, we prayed and praised, petitioned God for our countries, and requested that this peace of God that transcended all understanding would guard our hearts and minds in Christ Jesus. He did just that. Did our prayers change the threat? No. But they changed us in the midst of the threat.

This peace is a commodity our fear-ridden world is looking for. Peace is spoken of over 150 times in the Old Testament and over eighty times in the New Testament. Paul uses the word over forty times. Peace is something that enters the heart and makes it able to rise above all outside conditions.

Worry, in the end, disguises unbelief. And unbelief — coming to expression in a feeling of uneasiness or dread often related to negative thinking — takes us down, spoils our witness, and robs us of power to cope. Worry superimposes the future on the present and empties today of its strength.

Do you suffer from perpetual uneasiness? Do you have a chronic low-grade spiritual headache? You need to listen to Paul. Logic says that 10 percent of things you worry about actually happen —

and that leaves 90 percent of things you worry about that don't happen. Guess what I worry about? The 10 percent that will. The problem is that I waste today worrying about tomorrows that in most instances never come. Though logic can't keep me from worrying, God can. As J. B. Phillips writes in his translation of 1 Peter 5:6, "You can throw the whole weight of your anxieties upon him, for you are his personal concern." The secret of the spiritual art of serenity and its resulting freedom from anxiety starts and ends here — in God's loving arms.

QUESTIONS FOR REFLECTION AND DISCUSSION

1. Read Philippians 4:4–9. Which verse from this passage would you like to send to your friends and relatives? Why?

2. Read the quote below by Annie Dillard. What does she worry about? Can you relate to her concerns?

   I meant to accomplish a good bit today. Instead I keep thinking: Will the next generations of people remember to drain the pipes in the fall? I will leave them a note.*

---

*Annie Dillard, *Teaching a Stone to Talk* (1982; reissue, New York: HarperCollins, 1992), 167–68.

3. Read what I've written below. How do you cope with this fearmonger?

> Worry is Satan's tool. He is a liar, a murderer, a killjoy, who wants you worrying yourself to death. He will bring your past to mind as though it were today. He will bring tomorrow to your mind and play horror movies that have you as the main victim. He tells you that if you worry enough, you'll be able to stop whatever you fear will happen or to keep a situation from deteriorating. Remember: Satan has to stop you from turning the worrisome situations in your life over to God, from responding in such a way that you give glory to God. A healthy concern that acts and reacts responsibly and rightly in the situation engendered by the Spirit is *not* what Satan has in mind!

4. Look up and comment on the following verses: Matthew 6:25, 27–28; 1 Corinthians 7:32–34; 2 Corinthians 11:28; 1 Peter 5:7.

THOUGHTS FOR PRAYER

1. Pray for all your concerns. Put them in God's backpack. Enjoy the feeling of freedom.

2. Jot down some thoughts about what you've learned in this chapter. Form a prayer to God in which you summarize your response to this chapter.

CHAPTER 8

the spiritual art of
receptivity

My God will meet all your needs
according to his glorious riches in Christ Jesus.
Philippians 4:19

Paul knew how to give, but he also knew how to receive. That's an art—a spiritual art. To "receive" means "to take into one's possession something given or offered." It means "to accept." Some of us find it hard to be receptive. Yet the art of receiving graciously leads to spiritual blessing. Think of accepting the Holy Spirit into your life. Somehow it takes some of us a long time to simply say thank you and invite him to take over our lives.

To be able to accept all circumstances—hunger, deprivation, sickness, job loss, persecution, and so on—requires an act of faith. Yet, to accept the will of God in any and every situation leads to tranquillity of mind and soul, whatever that will is. When we accept what we cannot change, God gives us grace and peace to cope with it and also shows us how to receive his blessings along the way.

Philippians 4 contains one of my favorite Scripture verses: "I have learned the secret of being content in any and every situation" (4:12). Paul then lists some of those situations: when he is hungry and when he is full, when he has plenty and when he is in need.

I am still learning about the kind of contentment Paul describes. It is the ability to accept the unacceptable by receiving the grace God gives us to accept it. The art of receptivity begins here. It takes grace to receive God's provision, even in difficult and worrisome circumstances.

GRACE GIVERS AND RECEIVERS

Paul ends his letter to the Philippians with words about grace: "The grace of the Lord Jesus Christ be with your spirit" (4:23). He wants the grace of Jesus to be a reality in the lives of the people. "For you know the grace of our Lord Jesus Christ," writes Paul to the Corinthians, "that though he was rich, yet for your sakes he became poor, so that you through his poverty might become rich" (2 Corinthians 8:9). We should be like Jesus. Grace is dispensed through the Holy Spirit so that we can be givers of grace ourselves. It takes grace to be both a giver and a receiver—to give out of our means, whatever it may be, so that others may receive. It's a spiritual art.

When we served as youth workers in the United Kingdom, I remember a time when we had just a few pounds in the bank. We received very little salary to provide for ourselves and our three children. One day I realized I had ten pounds in my purse. A young boy came to see me to ask about attending our short-term training center—which required ten pounds to sign up for. He had no money at all. I struggled. How could I give him my ten pounds? And what if he couldn't find any more money for additional fees? That would not be a responsible thing to do. I gave him the money anyway.

That night a friend came to our little cottage to get a haircut. We all helped each other on the mission base, and this was my way of contributing. I had cut hair for years for free, but this night my friend said, "I need to pay you tonight, Jill." I protested, but she said, "No, I really feel I must—just this once." I practiced the art of receptivity. She opened her purse and pulled out a ten-pound note and put it into my hand. I laughed and shared my story with her. She was blessed to be the giver, and I was blessed to be the receiver. I discovered that you can't outgive God.

But what if it's impossible to be givers because we lack the basic necessities of life ourselves. What if we can't spread the gospel because there are no funds to print the Bibles or send the missionaries where they need to go? What if my needs aren't met, and therefore I can't meet other people's needs? You always have something to give, even if you are down to just offering a smile, providing a listening ear, or sharing a word of hope. Look around your life when you think you have nothing left to give. God will show you something you may have overlooked in your time of pain and need.

A CIRCLE OF GRACE

I have another favorite Bible verse from Philippians: "My God will meet all your needs according to his glorious riches in Christ Jesus" (4:19). This has to do with the art of receiving rather than giving—receive the fruit of people's generosity and practical help, and then you will have something to give to others who are worse off than you are. It's a circle of grace.

After Paul's initial needs were met by the churches in Philippi, Paul was able to brag on them when writing to the Corinthian believers. In 2 Corinthian 8:1–6, Paul reminds them of the reputation the churches in Macedonia have for generosity. He describes how God gave the churches grace while under severe trial so that from "their extreme poverty" they are able to give: "Out of the most severe trial, their overflowing joy and their extreme poverty welled up in rich generosity. For I testify that they gave as much as they were able, and even beyond their ability. Entirely on their own, they urgently pleaded with us for the privilege of sharing in this service to the saints" (8:2–4). Paul says that these believers "gave themselves first to the Lord and then to us in keeping with God's will" (8:5). Using the generosity of the Macedonian churches as an example, Paul urges the Corinthians to also "excel in this grace of giving" (8:7).

Do we plead with people for the privilege of giving to meet their needs, even out of our limited means? Paul says that we never give to God without receiving back. The Philippians have given beyond their means and now they are in need because of it (Philippians 4:14–18). Paul tells them that God is no one's debtor. God's bank is a bank that we cannot empty. We cannot draw down enough to bankrupt God. He is gloriously rich and has deposited those riches in Christ Jesus so we can never come to him in our need and have him say, "Sorry, there's nothing in the vault." There is a wealth of tranquillity there for the asking. Peace and joy are in the bank!

But we can also ask our heavenly Father to meet the basic needs of life as well as to provide for our spiritual necessities. When Jesus' disciples asked him to teach them to pray, he instructed them to ask for their "daily bread," for the material things they needed to live each day (Matthew 6:11).

Paul was a tentmaker. He provided for himself and his team with his own hands by making tents. But when he traveled for his mission work, he couldn't work, which meant that he was dependent on the practical help of other Christians. Now that he was in prison, he had no income at all. So the Philippians sent him funds by the hand of Epaphroditus (Philippians 4:18). And Paul received them graciously and gratefully—he said thank-you.

THE ART OF BEING A GOOD RECEIVER

This is one of the hardest arts of all for givers. I can tell you that I struggle to receive. As a doer, I find it difficult to let others "do" for me. Yet the Christian life revolves around learning the art of being a good receiver: "So then, just as you received Christ Jesus as Lord, continue to live in him" (Colossians 2:6). First we receive Jesus into our hearts by his Spirit. Then we "live in him." We continue on in the journey, drawing on his life within us. Then we receive his help in all areas of our life. He is our counselor and our friend.

Years ago, a dear friend lived with us while completing his doctorate in psychology at a local university. He was a wise man to whom God gave many wonderful gifts of help and healing. Before he moved in, he lived thousands of miles away. Although we didn't see each other very often, I would occasionally contact him to ask for advice on various matters, including challenges with raising kids. At the time he came to live with us, Stuart and I were raising three teenagers. Now that he was actually in our house, can you imagine how many times a day I strolled down to his flat to ask, "Do you have a minute for me?" He always did, and he helped me navigate some tough times.

When the Spirit of God comes into our lives, he moves in permanently. We can run to him at any time of the day or night because he lives here—right in our hearts. When we receive Christ, we *receive Christ*—the wonderful Counselor, the Prince of Peace, the Mighty God! In Christ we have received this wealth of resources.

So the Christian life begins by receiving Christ. Then it continues the way in which it began. We receive "everything we need for life and godliness" moment by moment and day by day (2 Peter 1:3). We have in our possession all things spiritual in him, but he also promised to answer prayers for our daily needs. As we receive spiritual blessings from Christ and through his people, we are to receive material blessings as well. This experience of giving and receiving material help should be going on in the church all the time.

The supply of God's servants rests on the generosity of God's servants. The Philippian believers responded to Paul's ministry in both spiritual and practical ways (see Philippians 4:14–16). They prayed for him. They were interested in his reports. They kept in touch at no small cost to themselves. They gave money, clothes, and shelter, and they met Paul's physical needs as best they could. It wasn't a case of "out of sight, out of mind." They practiced the spiritual art of generosity in practical ways. They had the gift of generosity and liberality.

"Oh, good," you say, "I don't have that gift. I just have the gift of receiving." Really? That's too easy to say. There is a special gift of giving (see Romans 12:8—"if [a person's gift] is contributing to the needs of others, let him give generously"), but *all* of us must give (just as there is a gift of evangelism but all of us must witness, and there is a gift of being able "to help others" [1 Corinthians 12:28] but all of us must be helpful). Paul gave of himself, and the Philippians gave back what they could in thankfulness. Paul graciously received their gifts, the tokens of their love, but only as he had given of all he had to them. All of us are called to do that.

GIVING AND RECEIVING GENEROUSLY

During a worship service I will sometimes hear a pastor pray before an offering is taken, "Lord, please receive these tokens of our love and thankfulness to you for all you have done for us." I wonder if our tokens (our "small change") say something about us. If what I give in the plate is a token of my love for God and my thankfulness for the cross, do I need to rethink the level of my gift and commitment?

We have to learn the art of generosity by practicing it. Just start and be generous—today, this week, at work, in the church, at home. Then begin to practice the spiritual art of receiving. Receive a spiritual blessing from God. Be thankful. Praise him for it. Then keep your senses alert to anyone trying to encourage you, help you, or give you something, however small it may be. Receive it graciously.

There is an art to saying thank-you. Start by just saying it. Make a list of people you need to thank—your parents, your friends, your boss. Who helped you when you were in school? Your teachers? Your youth leaders? Who invested in your life? Write a note. Just say thank-you, just as Paul did to the Philippians.

If you don't know what to say, try to be specific. Paul was. He lists the things he received from his friends for which he was thankful. "It was good of you to share in my troubles," he said (Philippians 4:14). Has anyone written you a timely letter when you were in trouble? Have they shared in your troubles? In what way? Did they stop by your home to comfort you when your parents died? Did they bring you chicken soup when you were ill? Did they help you pack and load boxes when you moved? Sit down and think about the help you received and write a letter, send an email, pick up the phone, or pay a visit. Just say thank-you.

Paul remembers that the Philippian church was the only church that gave support when he left Macedonia; he was supported financially by only one of the churches he planted. With gratitude in his heart, he acknowledges that these believers "sent [him] aid again and again when [he] was in need" (4:16). When Paul was in Thessalonica, no one fed him or sheltered him; no one gave to him. The church in Philippi heard about his need and continually sent him relief. The Philippian church was an "again and again" church. Are *we* "again and again" givers? If we are, we will find that we are continually receiving as well.

Paul reminds his readers that givers always end up receiving more than they give. "I am amply supplied" through the gifts you sent, he says (4:18), and now God will resupply you (4:19). He points out that God will credit their gift to their account in heaven (4:17). Did you know you have an account in heaven?

Do you know anyone in need like Paul was? Any missionaries who have lived for years on half their basic support? There are hundreds of these servants of the Lord. Perhaps you're thinking that there is so much need and you only have so much to give. Stretch a bit. Go out on a limb. Give even out of your poverty. There are trained missionaries who gave up lucrative marketplace jobs out of their desire to go to other countries to tell lost people about Christ, but they're unable to move an inch because they don't have the means to get there.

We have supported hundreds of these choice servants over the years, and in return we have received generous gifts from these servants of the kingdom. It was hard to receive such sacrificial gifts, but it was important we did so for their sake. We knew that God would reward them, and we didn't want to deprive them of that blessing. As Paul said, "I am looking for what may be credited to your account" (4:17).

All of us know such generous people. I think of women in my life who were amazingly generous with their time when I was a young Christian. I recall someone who took a night job to earn extra money to send me to Bible school. And I remember the missionary in sub-Saharan Africa who patiently and tenaciously defied an inhospitable wilderness climate to grow a small rosebush in a barrel. She generously cut three precious roses and gave them to me on my breakfast tray after I became sick when we visited them. I was feeling horrible, and there on my breakfast table were three cut roses. I cried!

I have met widows around the world who give their "mites" daily to help an AIDS mother or a starving adult in a disaster region. I have watched incredible sacrificial gifts at work as I serve with World Relief.

When Stuart and I served in a youth ministry for ten years in the United Kingdom, our income was well below that of the average wage earners around us. We, along with all the other missionaries, relied on donors to give to the work. It's an interesting experience to be dependent for your daily bread on church members who may or may not remember to put a dollar in the plate on Sunday or to send a donation to the mission. We didn't talk about money but were encouraged to ask the Lord to meet our needs. We never went hungry. God provided, and we learned to be receivers.

It was an adventure. I learned to be content and to pray for my daily bread and anything else we couldn't afford but needed. I began to learn the spiritual art of simplicity—to sort out what was a need and what was a want, and to depend on God alone. For me, having grown up in a well-off family, this was a big change.

I didn't do too badly with the basic things, but when it came to the work of the Lord, I had a steep learning curve. Why should

God's work lack resources? I began to get angry. Our youth ministry took over an old warehouse and turned it into a coffee bar as an outreach for the kids in the area. We gave all we could and began to pray for the rest. A lovely young woman gave up a good job so she could turn the shop at the end of the building into a Christian bookstore—the first for miles around. People donated books to help us get started and sent money to pay this woman's salary. Many gave of their time, their talents, and their furniture—bookshelves, desks, and even the cash box. Soon we had a thriving small business that paid for much of the work carried out with the young people of the town.

Meanwhile, I offered my skills as a teacher and started a preschool on one of the four floors in our ministry building. What began with nothing soon turned into a model school with over three hundred students. I worked for no pay for ten years and charged parents a minimal fee, and the school eventually provided enough money to develop the rest of the building for the youth ministry. It became a center for the gospel in the area.

Talk about generosity! People gave above and beyond their means. But that's what people do when they love the Lord and want to serve him.

We learned not only to live generously but to receive the generosity of others. So often we are meager in our giving. Paul talks about people who gave out of their poverty, not out of their abundance, and that's what the spiritual art of giving—and receiving—is all about.

A BIT AT A TIME

Giving your life away a bit at a time is a lifelong occupation. It starts with a full surrender to the will of God in your life—and doing so before you know what it entails. "Whatever, Lord; whenever, Lord; however, Lord" are good words to use. It is a mind-set that asks, "What do I possess that I did not receive?" A mind-set that is ever grateful for Jesus. A mind-set that regards everything I have as a trust for the kingdom. I am simply a steward, not only of the mysteries of God (1 Corinthians 4:1), but also of anything God gives me here and now to use for him. That includes my property, my home and garden, my cars, my bank balance, and so on. Everything. Jesus didn't say to the rich young ruler, "Leave some of it in escrow and follow me." He said, "Sell everything you have.... Then come, follow me" (Luke 18:22).

The amazing thing is that when you live like this, you find your own needs being met. Paul says to his generous friends in Philippi, "My God shall supply all your needs as you supply other people's needs. That's how it works. You supplied mine; God will supply yours" (Philippians 4:19, my translation).

I want my life to be characterized by generosity. I want people to see me giving it all, all the time, all the way. I want to because that's what Jesus did for me. "For you know the grace of our Lord Jesus Christ," says Paul, "that though he was rich, yet for your sakes he became poor, so that you through his poverty might become rich" (2 Corinthians 8:9).

When you know the grace of Jesus, then it's easy to respond in kind. Ask yourself: "How can I become poorer for Jesus?" This may not sit well in some circles today. I hear a lot of, "How can I become richer for Jesus?" Ask instead, "What can I give away? What would really cost me?" Do you get rid of all your loose change in the offering, or do you empty your purse into the plate and walk ten miles home because you have no money to pay for a bus ride, as a friend of mine did one day in response to a missionary offering? Extreme? Maybe. But did I hear a laugh? A great, grand cosmic laugh? Does God love the one who learns the spiritual art of generosity in all its dimensions? Oh yes, very much!

"Well, Jill," I hear you say, "I can't do that. That's taking this Christianity you talk about too far." It's a question of "*Will* you?" not, "*Can* you?" You can do anything God calls you to do. "Well," you say with relief, "God hasn't 'called' me to be irresponsible with money." True enough—God has simply asked you to give it all away. Come, follow him. Like the rich young ruler, you will go away sad if you refuse to abandon your life—all you have and all you are—to God. It's a choice. If you take the challenge, then you'll be able to say with Paul, "I can do everything through [Christ] who gives me strength" (Philippians 4:13).

HAPPY GIVING!

So whether it is the art of giving or the art of receiving, contentment comes when we are happy to do either, and it comes when we hold this world's goods lightly rather than tightly. We are content when we graciously and thankfully receive whatever worldly good the Lord provides. The beautiful promise, as Paul reminds us, is that "God will meet all your needs" (4:19). Notice that he doesn't say all your *wants*. We who live in the rich West sometimes get the two mixed up. In the end, the best things in life are free, and Paul concludes his letter to the Philippians by reminding them of God's priceless gifts that no amount of money can buy—things such as grace, and peace, contentment and spiritual blessings. May you revel in God's gifts and, of course, the gift of gifts—God's own dear self.

HOW TEACHABLE AM I?

There is one additional facet of the spiritual art of receptivity that Paul practiced—the art of teachability. "I have learned ... " says Paul (Philippians 4:11). What had he learned? Many things about God, about himself, and about lost people. He learned to live one day at a time in the power of Christ's life. He learned to use whatever happened to him and his companions as an opportunity for good and for God at any given time. He *learned*. He was *teachable*. And he was tenacious about both practicing and teaching the spiritual arts.

When Stuart and I first came to the United States from the United Kingdom in 1970, I was surprised by the emphasis I found in the evangelical world on the "how-tos" of the faith. In the United Kingdom, evangelical teaching was strong on principles and weak on practicality; it was clear on *what* we should do but vague on *how* to do it, heavy on proclamation but light on application. It was a challenge to get my mind around it all.

But balancing principles and practicality was never a problem for the great apostle Paul. Surely he was a master at both practice and proclamation. In his final chapter of this letter, he writes, "I have learned to ..." Though nearing the end of his life, he is still learning. "How about me? Am *I* still teachable?" I wondered as I began writing this last chapter of my book. I don't know how old the apostle was, but I know how old I am. I am seventy-two years of age. It would be tempting to think, "Surely I can coast at this point and live off the wealth of things I've already learned about Jesus and his love."

Then I come across Paul's prayer that we would have power to know the love of Christ that surpasses knowledge—to know the height of it, the depth and width of it, the scope of it (see Ephesians

3:18–19). Are there enough years in our little life span to know that? And is it possible to learn the how-tos of accepting the things you cannot change—like chains and deprivations—as well as how to cope with the times of plenty without growing fat and flabby?

It takes humility to stay teachable (remember chapter 3?). Jesus himself "grew in wisdom and stature, and in favor with God and men" (Luke 2:52). He grew and learned how to be fully human in every dimension. The author of Hebrews writes, "It was fitting that God, for whom and through whom everything exists, should make the author of their salvation perfect through suffering" (2:10). That is a learning process we experience from birth to death. There is something to learn every day of our lives. But we will not learn it if we are not developing the spiritual art of teachability.

SUBMISSION IS THE KEY

The dictionary defines "teachability," or someone who is "teachable," as being "willing and able to learn." The thought of our Lord being teachable—*learning* to be a man—takes my breath away. It's mind-boggling when you think about it. Jesus put himself into a situation in which he had things to learn. Yet he did it. And it is submission to the will of God that is the key to teachability.

"Submission" isn't a word over which I particularly want to linger. But in the end, we all submit to something. You cannot live as a human being without it. When you submit, you are abandoning your whole life to one end—to glorify God.

Teachability, our ability to be humble and submissive to the new things God wants to teach us, is the key to learning whatever lesson of the spiritual arts we must learn. Although each person who reads this book will likely zone in on one spiritual art above another, we all have to start at the same place to learn it. We must submit to the learning process—to the discipline of whatever it is we have to practice. It may be a good idea to pause even now and ask yourself, "What does God want me to learn from reading this book? Am I teachable? Am I willing to readily receive what he wants me to learn?"

PUTTING TEACHABILITY INTO PRACTICE

Learning new disciplines requires planning and setting aside time to submit to whatever it is these practices may require of us. In fact, a good first step is to take some time away to think about it. You might say, "But, Jill, I need God to teach me humility. How do I put *that* on my schedule?" Well, perhaps you could plan a mission trip where you get your hands dirty in a challenging project that requires compassion. This may mean setting aside other pursuits, such as learning to water-ski or taking a course to gain new skills in your vocation. Or it could be that you go to your pastor or other church leaders and ask that you be empowered to exchange leadership or teaching opportunities for following and serving opportunities for a period of time. It may mean you take a self-learning theological study on the Internet that will require submitting your life to some additional stress for a time. It is important that those who teach others also teach themselves. I don't know what it will require in your case, but carefully consider the art you need to learn, and then submit to whatever time it takes to learn it.

It may be a matter of learning a skill or a character trait— gentleness, for example. Can you learn how to be gentle? Yes, you can learn how to be anything God wants you to be if you are teachable. Ask yourself, "How can I practice this character trait in my life?" Well, look around for a difficult person in your life.

Most of us don't have to look far. Think of your past dealings with this person. Have you been harsh, loud, or bossy? Have you been inflexible and unwilling to change tactics? Try gentleness. How? Submit to the Spirit's working in you. Next time you talk to your difficult person, remember the Scripture that says, "A gentle answer turns away wrath, but a harsh word stirs up anger" (Proverbs 15:1). It doesn't mean that you allow this person to run all over you; it means you gently and firmly hold your ground, smile, and lovingly see that you are heard. That takes practice. But gentleness is a learned art.

They say old dogs can't learn new tricks. Well, I am an old dog, and I'm still learning new tricks—but only insofar as I submit myself to the learning process, admit that I need to learn whatever is necessary to make me more mature in Christ, and make sure that I learn the how-tos as well as the principles of daily Christian living.

PRAYER

As you ponder now the lessons of receptivity and teachability, you may wish to borrow these words as you offer your own prayer:

Lord, I want to learn the art of giving and receiving, as Paul and the Philippians did. First, I must practice receiving your spiritual riches. I need to walk around my world with my palms open to receive your grace and the love of all the saints as it comes to me. I need to receive graciously the words of thanks that come my way. But I also need to receive the word spoken in correction or rebuke when it is deserved. I need to humble myself to simply say thank-you and to mean it. Being receptive means being open to all your gifts on a daily basis. For this I need to be teachable, to submit to hearing and obeying your will for my life. For this I need the Spirit's help. And as I learn to receive, I also want to learn to be more generous—to be willing to give my all, because Christ has given his all for me. So here I am, Lord. Work all of these spiritual arts in me. Make me like Christ.

In Jesus' name. Amen.

QUESTIONS FOR REFLECTION
AND DISCUSSION

1. Read Philippians 4:10–20. Choose the verses that God is using to speak to you and then share them with others.

2. Discuss what it means to receive from God, from others, and from the church.

3. What is the most difficult part of receiving from others?

4. What does Paul teach you in Philippians 4 about the art of giving and receiving and being teachable?

5. What are you doing in your life to exercise a teachable heart?

6. What kinds of opportunities could you seek in the coming days to learn new things, which you can put into practice in very specific situations?

7. What does it mean to you to submit to God's will? Where in your life is it difficult to give control over to God and to surrender to his will?

THOUGHTS FOR PRAYER

1. Pray about the areas in your life where you don't feel contentment at present.

2. Pray for a teachable spirit that is open to receiving the Lord's provision for any areas of discontent that come to your mind.

3. Pray for an openness to see the opportunities—and to respond to them—to practice the art of generosity.

4. Pray for the courage to be submissive to the will of God in your life.

5. Take some time to review the spiritual arts discussed in this book. Which chapter has meant the most to you, and why? Spend some time praying about what you can do in response to what you have learned.

6. Pass on your book to another group to use.

epilogue

At the moment, I'm working on the art of "how to travel the world and live out of a suitcase." For the last six years, Stuart and I have been freed up by our church to be ministers at large, responding to invitations around the globe, particularly in the developing world where the church is growing rapidly. As I conclude this book, let me share a travel narrative of a recent trip that demonstrates how the spiritual arts often play out in my everyday life and ministry. I hope it will help you to see how the spiritual arts can play out in your life—and perhaps give you a better picture of what I mean about being "a teachable old dog"!

I was on my way to join Stuart on an international ministry trip. He had gone ahead of me to the Channel Islands and would proceed to India, where we would connect for the rest of the journey. Just a normal start to an overseas trip for both of us. Ahead were full days of travel and teaching—and challenges yet unknown.

My first challenge was trying to get out of Toronto to catch my Chicago connecting flight to India. After a three-hour delay sitting on the tarmac (chained to my airplane seat—a test of my patience, which I failed!), we took off and arrived just in time to catch the flight at O'Hare. In fact, I was the last to board. "There goes my luggage," I thought. Well, hadn't Paul said that he'd learned contentment in both plenty and want? I guess this trip would be a little test to help me learn how to be content with nothing.

As I found my seat and settled in for the long flight, I thought back over the last several days. While Stuart began this ministry tour in the Channel Islands, I began at Moody Bible Institute in Chicago, where I had been invited to speak at chapel and to spend time with students and staff. I love to be on a college campus, where students want me to sit in a dorm room or at the café and just have me talk—not *at* them but *with* them. The students pick the topics, and this time it was, "Tell us some of your life lessons."

More and more people are asking me to share my *long* life and the things I've learned in over fifty years of ministry—I wonder why! It could be because of my gray hair and the way I forget things all the time. Stuart says I'm like Christopher Columbus, who seems to have been famous for not knowing where he was going or where he was when he got there, and not having a clue where he had been when he got back. This interest in my long life may be because people reckon they had better get me to pass on what I know before I pass out!

Not long ago, I was more than a little miffed when a valet who parked my car at a country club where I was speaking at a missions fund-raiser asked, "Have you got everything from the car, Miss?" To which I replied, "Oh, I put my … my … my … "—and before I could think of what I *had* put on the backseat, he inquired helpfully, "Your *walker*, ma'am?" I was stunned. "My computer!" I snapped.

Anyway, I spent hours that day with groups of Moody students—many wonderful young people training for world ministry. It occurred to me that in the months or years ahead, I might even bump into one of these students in Asia, Africa, the Middle East or Europe.

I thought of Paul and the important investment he had made in Timothy. Paul taught this young man the spiritual arts, and Timothy in turn continued to teach them to others. My Moody experience was yet another confirmation of how important it is that we who are aging follow Paul's example by actively passing on our faith.

Stuart and I have had so many opportunities to reach, teach, inspire, and train the next generation for Christ. Thinking of this brought to mind the words of the psalmist:

> Since my youth, O God, you have taught me,
>> and to this day I declare your marvelous deeds.
> Even when I am old and gray,
>> do not forsake me, O God,
> till I declare your power to the next generation,
>> your might to all who are to come.
>
> Psalm 71:17–18

So here we are, busy doing just that, and God has not forsaken us as we travel and engage in training.

From Moody it was on to Toronto to join Anne Graham Lotz for a two-day "Just Give Me Jesus" arena event. After Anne's message on Friday night, hundreds of people poured into the aisles and onto the platform as an indication of their desire to accept Jesus as Savior and Lord. It was one of the most amazing responses to a message I had ever witnessed.

The next morning, I spoke at the mission services at the Peoples Church in Toronto. Pastor Charles Price introduced me as his youth leader from over fifty years ago and described how I had taken him with me when he was sixteen years old and thrown him into the deep end in street ministry. That, he said, was where his evangelism training had begun. I had no idea! (God reminded me, as he reminded Paul, that pouring one's life into a young Timothy—in my case, a young Charles—is just as important as speaking to a huge crowd in Athens.)

It was on his travels that Paul met the men who became invaluable ministry partners—Luke, Epaphroditus, Timothy. I am still trying to practice this same spiritual art, looking for the individuals whom God strategically places in my path. However, this is not an art that requires an international journey. You can be aware of the people around you on your domestic journeys as you travel to the grocery store, the doctor's office, and church. Stay alert for the people whom God is intentionally bringing into your life.

I left Toronto the next day and arrived in India during the middle of the night. As I suspected, my luggage hadn't made it. Nevertheless, I had an unexpected and delightful day with Stuart in Hyderabad—unexpected because I was supposed to travel directly to Bangalore and then back to Hyderabad to join Stuart a week later. As it turned out, Bangalore had declared "a ban"—an entire city shutting down as a protest of one thing or other, and woe to anyone who dares to venture outside or to work for any reason. For me, this meant a great day with Stuart, with a couple of meetings thrown in with the Operation Mobilization leaders Stuart was training.

Jet lag notwithstanding, I managed to stay awake at least while I was talking, and the delay allowed my luggage to catch up with me. Can you imagine the lengths God goes to care for me? It took a citywide shutdown to ensure that I had my bags—which contained all my teaching notes for five weeks of ministry! Incidentally, Lufthansa had given me a wad of money when I arrived in India. They obviously didn't expect my bags to turn up, and they said I would need to buy clothes and other things. That money took care of most of our personal expenses while we were in India. God is good—all the time! It was yet another confirmation that my God will meet my needs—spiritual and physical.

I had a very stretching week with the leadership delegates from the Methodist Church and the United Church of South India (which includes all of the mainline denominations—think World Council of Churches). It was a first for these two large church bodies to combine for a joint convention. All the bishops from the different provinces sat on the front row, with the key women from every one of their churches in rows behind them. It took some effort not to feel intimidated.

Sometimes I taught for six hours a day in a hot and crowded setting, and I spent not a few days being a little out of sorts because of the food—nothing, of course, like Paul experienced in a hot, stuffy cell eating prison fare, but enough of a challenge to force me to lean on God to supply the power to be tenacious and press on.

After a week of fighting jet lag and the heat, not to mention adjusting to pungent spices and debating theological issues with a few liberal church leaders (exhausting!), I rejoined Stuart, who had been training pastors at the Operation Mobilization headquarters in Bangalore. We then headed for Amritsar, the city of Sikhs in Punjab, North India. Here we had to quickly adapt to a huge culture shift as we spoke to Dalits—the untouchables—who are the lowest echelon of people in India. It is among these people that OM has planted fifteen hundred Good Shepherd churches and schools in the last five years.

We met with the leaders of these new churches and their spouses for an amazing week of teaching—with interpretation, which doubles our stress and halves our material. (I wondered how

Paul coped with the languages he encountered!) I resorted to a diet of rice, bananas, and bottled water, kept well and talked on.

Our venue was a wedding hall, but not with all the amenities you might think would come with such a place. Imagine an unventilated warehouse with no air-conditioning—hot, hot, hot—plus exhaust fumes billowing in from the motorbike park outside. Toss in incredible decibels of blaring traffic and music played louder than loud, as well as adults and kids wandering all over the place all the time, and you'll have just a glimpse of the place. Now imagine what it's like to try to teach the Bible over this hullabaloo for hours on end. Oh, and also consider the fact that some of these folk are illiterate, and you really get the picture—and the challenge. But it's nearly impossible to explain the privilege and joy it was to offer a shoulder to cry on and a helping hand to meet practical needs, to provide informal biblical teaching, and to encourage the OM teams—some made up of teenagers and twentysomethings. The women's teams, made up of young Indian women, routinely walk into unreached Sikh towns and Hindu villages, knock on doors, and start churches from scratch. It is dangerous and difficult evangelism, but OM tells us these indigenous women are great church planters in this culture. They have smiles that would charm a duck off water, hearts on fire for God, and courage that puts us to shame. But they are also what they are—young vulnerable women who were worn down and needed a break from living in difficult circumstances where they ate what they could and dealt with opposition that occasionally got violent. What a joy to encourage, love, and pray for them! I was glad for the opportunity, albeit short, to meet them, serve them, and learn from them. *It doesn't get much better than this!*

Kazakhstan was the next stop on our journey. Don't feel bad if you need the help of a globe—I did (remember Columbus). I had to pore over a map on the plane to figure out where on earth we were going. We had actually been there about ten years ago, and it was a difficult visit. So I was glad to be back and to find an amazing difference in the city of Almaty.

We hardly recognized it as the same place. Wealth generated from the country's abundant supplies of oil and natural gas has caused a profusion of high-rise buildings, fancy cars, and shops with luxury goods. (Sadly, the same wealth has also produced a fair amount of corruption and political intrigue.) There were shopping malls with knockoffs such as "King Burger," "Domino Doughnuts," and "The American University" (no American anything connected to it).

Cars clog the streets, and you can *buy* a driver's license here. No need to pass a test — a fact the crazy and dangerous drivers confirm. To get around, one just stands by the side of the road and hitches a ride with any citizen who stops. You then negotiate a price and, if acceptable, get in and hopefully get to your destination — more or less in one piece. Makes for an interesting commute!

Yes, change has definitely come to Almaty. Materialism rules. Local churches struggle to stem the tide. The Islamic government and the residue of atheistic culture from a Communist past do not make for a welcoming environment for the gospel.

Almaty is the capital city, and, while not like the great city of Rome in Paul's day, we had an opportunity to meet believers in both "Caesar's household" and those from the humbler classes who were new converts to Christianity. What joy to teach the spiritual arts of intimacy with God and serenity of mind to the future leaders of the church in Kazakhstan. We were amazed to see how the spiritual arts of humility and teachability were evident in these emerging leaders. Humility clothed their spirits, and they sat for hours, drinking in the teaching.

Attending our weeklong training were Kazaks, Uzbeks, Tajiks, Turks, Tatars, and various other ethnic groups from the former Soviet republics. Church leaders, pastors, and their spouses, came from all over this huge region. Some were highly educated and biblically trained; others were simple folk—farmers and shopkeepers. Despite the ill winds against them, these leaders are shepherding courageous and growing churches in their hometowns. They asked us to teach about Christian values in family and ministry, church leadership, prayer, and spiritual formation. Sometimes our talks were translated simultaneously into Kazak and Russian.

At the end of the week, they prayed for us (loudly and in unison) with their arms around us, some with eyes filled with tears. They prayed that God would bring us back to the extreme northern sections of the country, where many of them live and where they would gather all the churches in those remote areas so we could teach couples how to have a healthy marriage (there is much spousal abuse in this culture, even among Christian couples) and tell them the Bible stories we had taught here. Then, as is their habit, tough-looking but tenderhearted Uzbeks and Turks came to Stuart and asked him to pray over them. One man, tears streaming down his cheeks, shook with emotion and hung on to Stuart, not wanting to let him go. The man's brothers went to find him a handkerchief. It was profoundly moving. Meanwhile, I held babies and prayed over the women and children. *Hey, it doesn't get much better than this!* We hated to leave our new sisters and brothers in the faith, but they sent us on our way with grace—just as Paul had sent his dear ministers on their way.

We learned yet again that a ministry of "presence" counts for so much. We could send our books—and we do. We could send our tapes—and we do. We could recommend excellent Bible studies and leadership training manuals—and we do. But over and over again, they say, "You came! *You* came! You *came!*" That's called a ministry of presence. There's nothing quite like it.

So we prayed, taught, cradled babies, prayed for their sick, and struggled through the language barriers to listen to their hearts. We didn't want to leave, but I realized again that we were to show the spiritual art of maturity by letting go of our ministry for the sake of others, just as Paul did. We spent time with these modern-day equivalents of Epaphroditus, Timothy, and Luke. They would build on the little we were able to contribute.

So now we are into the last ten days of this ministry tour. We are in Krasnodar, Russia, with our dear friends Diane and Bryan Thomas, who founded a language school as well as a church plant-ing and training ministry here. We are repeating all of our teach-ing with leaders and pastors from all over the former Soviet Union. They represent tiny groups of new believers in Muslim strongholds such as Azerbaijan and Georgia. The stories they tell blow our minds. Here we seem to step back into the Acts of the Apostles as we hear how "the Lord is working with them" in amazing ways.

But here, too, these brave men and women are human. They are perplexed by things such as church disunity and wounded by family betrayal (those who convert to Christianity are disowned, or worse, by their families). They struggle to know how to reach unreached regions and are tired and worn down from the battle. Some come from Chernobyl, whose government failed to move them after the nuclear disaster when they were children, and now these young men and women suffer a range of physical ailments, including cancer and organ failure. One wonderful young pastor is going to Pakistan for a kidney transplant next month that could save his life, but here he is in the training center, determined to serve the Lord until he can't stand up any longer. (He reminded us of Epaphroditus!)

We are humbled by these sisters and brothers who desire to learn how to better serve the Lord they love in the midst of the difficult and dangerous environment in which they live and work. They shouted, "Christ is our life, and death is gain!" I told Stuart, "I want to be like them when I grow up."

Last night we had an impromptu meeting with thirty or so young African medical students who are at the university here on scholarships. I thought of Psalm 71 again. This was a "God serendipity" we didn't expect. I love the opportunities that abound on these trips. This is what the spiritual art of ministry is — recognizing and responding to the mission field that is between your own two feet at any given time. We had a fabulous time with these future medical leaders from Nigeria, Zimbabwe, and Kenya. Paul's Dr. Luke would have loved it!

They asked us to talk about the spiritual arts — intimacy with God, tenacity, serenity in a very difficult environment, and the ministry of reaching their fellow students for Christ. They asked, "How do we minister? How do we stay teachable? Tell us about the art of humility so we can receive all that God has for us in this place."

Saturday we return to London for two days and then head home for stateside ministry. Stuart leaves again shortly for South America, and then both of us go to Egypt before Christmas. We are thankful that God allowed us to be together for most of this trip. What a joy! (Plus, Stuart tells me where I am, where I've been, and where I'm going next!)

We know that the prayers offered for us on this trip have been abundantly answered. We know it's because our beloved kids and grandkids are praying for Papa and Nana. Or it's someone in the United States, the United Kingdom, or Singapore. Or perhaps our new friends among the poorest of the poor in India, or the brand-new sisters and brothers we just left in Kazakhstan. Or it could be the dozens of church planters gathered in Krasnodar on their knees on our behalf. We are rich beyond measure! How could we not be doing "just fine"? Like Paul's friends, our friends prayed for us; and like Paul, we prayed for our friends and family, new and old. We are so grateful for all the prayer work on our behalf.

The experience of practicing and teaching the spiritual arts simultaneously is a double blessing, of course. But then our teaching could have no power at all unless we were doing both—integrating our personal experience of the Christ, who is our life, with our ministry. So, like Paul, we "press on toward the goal to win the prize for which God has called [us] heavenward in Christ Jesus" (Philippians 3:14).

the spirit's art

Is Christ my life, and death my gain?
Can I say this like Paul?
Is all my focus "Christ alone,"
And he my all in all?
Or is my heart divided still
Between the things I own
And Christ, who is my Savior,
Who watches from his throne?

What does it really mean to show
Forth Christ within my life?
Will this affect what happens
And protect me from all strife?
Or will I ask for trouble
And bring suffering my way?
Will putting Jesus first affect
My destiny each day?

Will first things first mean harmony
Among the ones I lead?
Will being chained to Jesus
Give me everything I need?
Will Christ deal with my ego
And reduce me down to size,
So all will see me run the race
Straining for the prize?

The goal and purpose of a life
That wants to know him more
Should drive me near the heart of God
And all he has in store.
Lord, teach me some maturity,
The will to learn and grow,
In prayer and word and ministry
To see the Spirit flow.

So to a world of pain that needs
A peace of mind that's rare,
May people see me live content,
May people see his care.
May peace that passes knowledge fill
My troubled heart with grace,
Till, oh, one day when all is done
I'll see him face-to-face.

So, Lord, please work your art in me
Until transformed I'll be.
So death is gain, and Christ is life
For all eternity!